FOREST CAMERA
A Portrait of Ashdown

Peter Kirby

Foreword by Barbara Willard

Edited by Rosalind Bowlby

Sweethaws Press

Published in 1998 by

SWEETHAWS PRESS
OWL HOUSE
POUNDGATE
SUSSEX TN22 4DE
Telephone: 01892 653722

Reprinted 1999

Designed and typeset by
RSB Typesetters, St Johns, Woking, Surrey

Printed and bound in Great Britain by
Biddles Ltd, Guildford, Surrey

ISBN 0 9511 795 5 1

A CIP catalogue record for this book is
available from the British Library.

To my grandchildren Jacob and Jessica and all grandchildren of Ashdown Forest. I hope these words and photographs give some feeling of how your ancestors lived, and encourage you all to search for more than this book contains.

LIST OF ILLUSTRATIONS

Four generations of the Kirby family stand outside the Nutley primary school they all attended.
From left to right: Toby Kirby, Ross Tippett, Fred Kirby and Peter Kirby.

Introduction

My family first came to the Forest in 1884 when my great grandfather, Samuel Kirby, took up the post of Head Keeper to Sir John Shelley on his Maresfield Park Estate. His fourth son, Herbert, was my grandfather who worked on the estate for nineteen years before he was appointed Forest Ranger by the Board of Conservators in 1912 which began a family association with the Forest which was to span two generations and more than eighty years. On his retirement in 1948, Herbert became Manor Reeve to Earl De La Warr and continued in this post until 1961 when my father, Fred, succeeded him, a position that meant a great deal to him and it was a source of disappointment and regret that it passed out of his family when the Forest changed hands in 1988.

I was born in 1938 and brought up on Ford's Green, Nutley, in the house Herbert had moved into in 1912 and where I still live today. As a boy growing up in a village in the 1940s, I was surrounded by an older generation of men who had fought in the First World

War, all the young men were away in the Forces. As soon as I was old enough, I would go into the pubs and listen to the tales of the past, and when my grandfather showed me albums full of old photographs and the old school portraits in particular made me realise that these were the fathers and grandfathers of the people I knew, I listened to the stories these old men had to tell, pored over any old photographs they had, and copied them where I could. And so began an interest which I retain to this day, a fascination with the past which has resulted in a collection of some 1,000 photographs which depict over a century of rural life. I have a good retentive memory which has been useful when remembering the anecdotes told to me over fifty years ago in the drinking houses around the village (tales of poaching and old war exploits being my favourites), and some of these I have included in this book which weaves the story of Ashdown into a social history of the Forest and its villages at the turn of the last century. I have ended the book at the outset of the First World War; in our isolated rural communities life had remained much the same for hundreds of years, but the events of 1914 were to change things forever.

Where I can I have drawn extensively on contemporary memoirs and in particular those of Harry Walter and the Reverend Harry Peckham of Nutley; avid chroniclers of their day whose contributions give a sharp and vivid insight into life one hundred years ago.

I would like to express my sincere thanks to Beryl Easton for all her research at the Public Records Office on my behalf, and with whom I spent many happy evenings laying out the bones of this book. She kept me going when I felt like giving up, transcribing my rough notes into an initial draft for the final text. For her written input into what has become 'Forest Camera', I offer my gratitude.

I would also like to thank all those people who have given or lent me their photographs and allowed me access to their family albums, in particular Mr & Mrs Brian Gregory, Mr Stuart Braid, the late Mrs Nellie Keeys, the Keeley family, Mrs Vera Riley and family, Nutley W. I. and all the people of the villages who have given their time to talk to me and allowed me to copy their photographs. To those people whose photographs have not appeared or whose names have not been mentioned, please bear with me as another book is planned. I would also like to thank Gordon Turner for all his help with the photographs and from whom I learnt all I know about copying old prints, the late Barbara Willard for all her encouragement and for the Foreword she gave me permission to use before she died, and my editor and publisher, Rosalind Bowlby for all her research and work on the text. But finally I would like to dedicate this book to my father, Fred, and my grandfather, Herbert, the two people who had such a profound influence on my life, whose encyclopaedic knowledge of the Forest, its habitat and the people who lived on and around it remains unrivalled.

Peter Kirby
Nutley, 1998

Editor's Note

The editor would like to thank the following for their help: Eric C. Byford, Chris Marrable, John Linton, Mike Parcell, William Bell, Dave Arthur, editor of 'A Sussex Life: Memories of Gilbert Sargent Countryman', a new edition of which is now available, Mrs Margaret Bishop for plate 152, and the Friend family for the use of the jacket photographs of Thomas Friend.

Foreword

Plantagenet forethought is to be thanked for the existence today of Ashdown Forest, in the high wealden country of East Sussex. Alarmed by the advance of agriculture, with its felling and ploughing, King Edward III decreed the enclosure of nearly 14,000 acres; but this early act of conservation was not exactly altruistic. The enclosure was to be a royal *chace* where game, beleaguered by man's progress, might find shelter and breed freely – to be slaughtered in due course by merry huntsmen.

Seven centuries later, this slice of Sussex remains bound by ancient law. At the beginning its lords were kings; later it was given to the lords of the manor of Duddleswell, the Sackville family, the earls and dukes of Dorset.

Since then responsibility for the Forest has passed to a trust sponsored by the East Sussex County Council. Day to day management remains with the Board of Conservators, set up a century ago.

Ashdown has been described as a forest without trees. Today's experts, however, define the word forest according to the ground itself rather than its vegetation: Dartmoor, for example, is named as a forest on the Ordnance Survey map. Ashdown today is mostly open heathland, for its trees were under pressure for centuries. Apart from a royal practice of rewarding good service with gifts of timber, Ashdown was a site of the wealden iron industry for 300 years or so, its timber felled during clearance or for charcoal burning.

Look from an old map of Ashdown to one of today and you will see that its perimeter remains basically the same. Within the ancient pale (or fence), long tumbled, much is changed. The original acreage has been reduced, by history, greed and many enclosures. Its origins may lie in the gift of kings, but its maintenance over the centuries is due to the pig-headed customary tenants or Commoners who would not relinquish their privileges, so old that their origins are lost. Their Right of Common – which attaches to the ground, not the individual – allows them to graze their animals according to the size of their holding and cut certain timber, together with bracken or brakes for their beasts.

Four parish boundaries meet on the Forest: Hartfield with its timber framed houses and shingle spired church, Withyham, where the Sackvilles lived and where they are commemorated by some of the finest sculptors of the day in the local church, famous for its Sackville chapel, Maresfield and Buxted. Nutley is in the parish of Maresfield and has always been important to the Forest, but it is now a straggling roadside village, cut in two by the A22 London to Eastbourne road. It was on Ashdown Forest that A.A. Milne set his tales of Winnie the Pooh and his mates. The original Poohsticks Bridge is on the edge of the Forest and Pooh might well be counted among the Forest fauna – his devotees certainly find him more relevant than deer or fox, badger or coney.

Whatever Ashdown may lack it is not atmosphere; to experience its mysterious influences every day of the year is privilege indeed. And not only the soft seasons induce this magic, which persists even on the beastliest winter day; days without colour, when no bird flies and the far downs are shrouded in extravagant distance and facelessness. The place looks its more conventional best in autumn, when great strands of heather are almost matched by sheets of auburn bracken.

Land such as Ashdown will always suffer from fire; burning by accident is probably inevitable, and burning for fun may stem from the days when enclosure fences were furiously fired. Fires happen in the spring, when the bracken lies dead and exhausted and the grasses blow in dry, unnumbered swathes. As dark comes down, a spurt of flame will turn in seconds to a leaping blaze.

Some years ago, when the fire brigade could be slow in arriving, those of us living on the waste-edge of the Forest would rush out with beaters and fight as long and as hard as needed. There was a feeling of dedicated ownership about the practice. To save what was so cherished seemed well worth ashes in the hair, smoke in the eyes and horribly stinking clothes - worth it all anyway for those long in love with this place.

Barbara Willard

Nutley

Nutley was one of the woodland villages that evolved on the waste-edge of the Forest in the 13th century. It was recorded as early as 1249 and the name comes from Hnut, the Anglo-Saxon for a nut tree, and Leag, a forest glade or clearing abounding in hazel. By 1333, the settlement had become a series of farms and smallholdings, and the earliest recorded photographs of Nutley, taken over 100 years ago, show many more forest dwellings than there are now. They show, too, hops growing, and brick fields - small industries that have quite vanished from the place. And strange ragged characters under rough shelters, barefooted children, bearded tinkers. There was great poverty and loneliness, the road was small, dusty and winding, and at the inn on the corner the landlord would give you a pint of beer just to get you to stay and talk to him. The Uckfield and District Guide Book, published in 1869, carries the following description of Nutley: 'Numbers of little cottages may be counted below in the valley, each with cowhouse, garden, orchard, and one or two little crofts, green and flourishing, and all cribbed from the waste.'

Tradition claims that Edward II had a palace or hunting lodge near Nutley. Such places were, according to ancient opinion, 'the sanctuary and special delight of kings where, laying aside their cares, they withdraw to refresh themselves with a little hunting; there, away from the turmoils inherent in a court, they breathe the pleasures of natural freedom.' We know that, in 1324, he executed two deeds and wrote several letters, all headed 'Our Palace at Mersefeld'; medieval documents suggest that this royal residence could have been in the Millpond area of Maresfield. Others lay claim to Vachery Wood: 'The ruins of John of Gaunt's Castle are still to be seen in Vechery Wood' pronounced the Rev. C.N. Sutton in 1902, writing in his 'Historical Notes of Withyham, Hartfield and Ashdown Forest'.

According to local tradition, it was during these visits that the King paused on high ground north of Duddleswell while herds of deer were driven before him, hence the name King's Standing - the hunter's station from which to shoot game. Variations of the tale involve other monarchs. The whereabouts of the royal hunting lodge has attracted much attention, and as such a residence was bound to have had attendant buildings, one of them a chapel, there is one recorded as the Free Chapel of Notlye which probably served it. This 'wayside chapel', thought to date from Saxon times, was by an ancient track in an area which is known to this day as Chapelwood. In 1372, the chapel was included in the gift of the 13,391 acres of the Chase of Ashdown granted by Edward III to his third son, John of Gaunt, Duke of Lancaster, in return for some lands in Yorkshire, and for the next three hundred years it was known as Lancaster Great Park. John of Gaunt was patron to the reformer, John Wycliffe, who is said to have sought refuge in the district and officiated there, and it is possible that Wycliffe worked on his translation of the Bible in this very chapel, fashioning his great phrases for the King James's version as he walked through the Forest. The 1869 Uckfield Guide states boldly:

'It is highly probable that the great Protestant Reformation began from the Free

Chapel of Notlye. The Flemings and the Frenchmen who came into Sussex as iron workers, glass makers and cloth weavers sent word home to the Continent; the tree of life rooted and grew; Huss ate and lived, and a hundred years afterwards Martin Luther made his memorable journey to Rome, as our Wycliffe had done in 1374; and then the Reformation began indeed. The Elector of Saxony was to Luther what John of Gaunt had been to Wycliffe'.

The chapel was no longer in use in 1541 after the Reformation, although the ruins survived into the eighteenth century. The ancient font was discovered about 1800 beneath two feet of soil; it was lost again and rediscovered half a century later serving as a cattle trough on a local farm. The then Rector of Maresfield removed it to his church, where it remains, despite efforts to bring it to Nutley Church which some consider should be its resting place. Nutley village did not have a church until 1847, when the ecclesiastical parish was formed out of the parish of Maresfield; St. James the Less was built of stone in the Early English style, its architect R.C. Carpenter was better known as the man who designed Lancing College. An aisle was added in 1871.

1. Arthur Francis 1890

Arthur Francis was a photographer who lived in Nutley; his photographs depict rural life at the end of the nineteenth century and present a social history of the area as vivid as the written word. Born in Middlesex on 7 April 1855, only twenty years after William Henry Fox Talbot had invented the negative-positive process of photography with a camera developed by him from a camera obscura, his birth certificate shows his father, Charles, to be a Master Hairdresser, although he was also a professional photographer and probably took this portrait of his son.

When Arthur Francis came to Nutley around 1890, he had moved from Abergavenny in Wales where the family had lived since he was a child. He had two sons, Harry and Alfred, by Caroline Stevenson of Nutley, although there is no record of their wedding. Caroline, some twenty years his junior, was known as Tiny Bob, thought to derive from a mannerism.

It is not known why Arthur moved to Nutley, but he remained there, living in The Shanty at the end of the row of buildings in the high street in which officers had been billeted during the Napoleonic Wars, still residential and known to this day as The Barracks. With his camera he travelled in and around Nutley and the nearby villages bordering Ashdown Forest, recording a world that had changed very little for many hundreds of years. He was also Nutley's last lamplighter, lighting up the paraffin street lamps at dusk; they were kept going by public subcription until the Great War. Caroline had left him to care for the children of her younger son, Alfred, who lived in Penge, although she sometimes visited Nutley, bringing the children to see their grandfather. One of his granddaughters remembers him 'as a Father Christmas figure, and a bit of a gentleman.' My father, Fred Kirby, remembered him as an old man with a long white beard that he used to tuck into the top of his trousers.

Arthur Francis died in 1934 at the district workhouse in Uckfield, then called the Uckfield Union, which indicates that he was not well off in old age. The fear among countryfolk was that, when old age overtook them, they might be forced, through poverty, infirmity or both, to leave their cottages for the workhouse which was not merely distressing and uncomfortable, but felt to be a terrible disgrace. He is buried in Uckfield cemetery.

2. The Barracks 1890

Arthur Francis lived in The Shanty, the single-storeyed end of The Barracks, and would hang any photographs he wanted to sell outside on the wooden fence.

3. Nutley High Street 1880

The view of the High Street is taken from outside The Barracks on the left of the picture, looking north beyond the entrance to Bell Lane and up to the gate and wall of Nutley Church, lined by the great elm trees which were felled in the 1920s.

4. Chestnut Farm 1888

Looking east from Ford's Green, Chestnut Farm lies in the valley below Lower and Upper Misbourne, seen here on the right and left hand side of the horizon respectively. This photograph shows the open nature of the Forest at that time; the trees of Ashdown had been felled over the centuries to fuel the Wealden iron furnaces that burned until the last foundry closed in the early nineteenth century and Britain's iron industry moved to the Midlands where the cheaper fuel, coal, replaced charcoal. The scars left upon Ashdown's landscape prompted William Cobbett to write in January 1822: 'At about three miles from Grinstead you come to a pretty village called Forest Row, and then, on the road to Uckfield, you cross Ashurst (sic) Forest, which is a heath, with here and there a few birch scrubs upon it, verily the most villainously ugly spot I ever saw in England. This lasts you for five miles, getting, if possible, uglier and uglier all the way, till, at last, as if barren soil, nasty spewy gravel, heath and even that stunted, were not enough, you see some rising spots, which instead of trees, present you with black, ragged, hideous rocks.'

Sixty-six years after that blot on its landscape, the Forest had regenerated into open moorland where commoners excercised their rights to graze their animals and cut brakes and litter - bracken, heather and gorse - for winter bedding for them, and thatching for roofs, and to cut estovers - birch, alder and willow - for fuel, thus keeping saplings and other growth down.

Chestnut Farm and its neighbour up the track are still there today, although the house behind it was demolished in the 1890s. On the horizon, the clump of trees at Camp Hill can been seen indistinctly.

5. The Cottage of Tinker Wright 1888

Tinker Wright, seen here standing by the window of his cottage, was a well-known local character, adept at enclosing, or 'cribbing', parts of the Forest . The traditional grab enclosure consisted of a ditch and bank, with a roof of thatched heather and a smoking chimney, all completed within twenty-four hours; 'If this goes on I shall have an Indian town close to me of some of the greatest rapscallions that ever existed,' wrote an exasperated Sir John Shelley from his Maresfield Estate in 1826.

In his Reminiscences, Harry John Peckham, Vicar of Nutley from 1882-1913, writes:

"James Wright, commonly called 'The Tinker', was a real character. He originally came from 'some shire', and squatted on Ashdown Forest, where from time to time he enclosed an acre of ground and built a hut upon it. This he afterwards sold and bought a very small enclosure, only a few rods in extent, and built a hut of matchboard supported on posts over the ditch which bounded it. In this room he and his family, wife, two or three sons, and a grandchild lived, whilst the donkey and barrow lived underneath. It was said that the contract price for this mansion was 10s., and as a shelter it was dear at the price, for the matchboarding warped and you could see the sky above and the earth (or the donkey) beneath. The Sanitary Inspector one day reported it to the District Council as not having sufficient cubic feet of air for the inhabitants but, as one member of the Council remarked, 'you might just as well talk of the cubic contents of a birdcage'. One winter's day he said to me: 'You would have laughed if you had been in my place this morning. I always sleeps in an old billycock hat, and this morning when I woke, bothered if my head wasn't jammed tight. It had snowed in the night and come through the cracks, and my head and my hat and the wall was all froze together solid, and I was forced to tear the old hat before I could get my head out'. Mrs Peckham knitted him a helmet to replace the spoilt billycock.

He was an adept at forest encroachment, and his house, which was built over the boundary ditch, soon appeared in the middle of his ground. I said to him one day 'Tinker, I never saw a little place grow like yours does', to which he replied 'You know my old donkey? Well, he is dead, and as no fence could keep him in or out when he was alive, I wonder what he will do now he is dead. So I buried him in the middle of the plot, and bothered if he isn't hucking the fences out all round'. The Forest Ranger reported the encroachment, and he had to appear before the Bench, where I believe he told the same tale; but he had to undo the donkey's work."

It was standard practice for a forester to increase his smallholding by nibbling away at the boundary, fencing a haystack at night for example, or moving a fence to include a faggot or turf stack placed outside; by the morning he would claim this grab enclosure as his own and a small fee would be paid to the Lord of the Manor at the next Court Baron to mark that the ground had been 'sot in' or 'set in'. In 1885 an Act of Parliament put an end to the lawless activites of Tinker and his fellows when a Board of Conservators was established to oversee the bye-laws of the Forest and to protect the rights of its Commoners, some 100 in number. The Act also recognised the endeavours of the cribbers and decreed that all those who could establish that they had owned land on the Forest before 9 December 1869, however acquired, could retain it free of charge. Those who had enclosed since that date could buy at a fair market price. Needless to say, there were some strange sales: a family who had enclosed 17 separate plots retained them for £88; Albert Turner of Nutley was happy to pay the same price for his one and a quarter acres.

Altogether, 156 enclosures of thirty-three and a half acres were found to have been made by 104 persons, and the ground was sold to them for £1,018 16s 9d. Tinker's hut was demolished after that and a house, still known as Lavender Cottage, was built on the site by Nelson Turner.

6. Tinker Wright 1880

This portrait by Arthur Francis was reproduced as a postcard, and written on the back of the original, in the hand of Harry Walter, was the following:

'This is a photograph of James Wright who we knew as the old Tinker. He and his family came and squatted on the forest at a place called the Tinkers Hole about 1875, his eldest two sons encroached 2 plots on the forest now known as Ardens and Little Birches. He later bought a plot of land near the parish field and erected a wooden shack on it about 1884 and lived there until his death in July 1895 and is buried in Nutley Churchyard. He had a family of 4 sons and 3 daughters.'

The Reverend Harry Peckham recalls:

'Mrs Wright told me that one of her babies had been born ruptured and that she had tried the usual remedy, to split an ash sapling and pass the child through it and then bind up the tree with hay bands. If the tree grew together the child would be cured, and vice versa. In her case this was left doubtful as someone cut down the tree . . . Notwithstanding the lack of cubic space in his house and his Scriptural objection to beer (and all alcohol), the Tinker lived several years over 80; he used to sit in his chair, and if he was not watched he would light a piece of shavings underneath it; and it speaks well of Mrs Tinker that he died in his bed at last. He used to chew tobacco and Spanish licorice mixed, which he carried in a tin box shaped like a coffin, his own handiwork.'

7. Ivy Cottage, Ford's Green 1887

This tiny, ivy covered cottage was the focus for the activities of the members of the local Rat and Sparrer club, who would arrive at night when the sparrows were roosting and throw a fine mesh net right over the top of the dwelling. They would then beat the ivy with sticks to drive out the birds which were then caught in the net and killed. There was a bounty of one penny per sparrow. The same method was used for driving rats from local hay and corn stacks, when a bounty of two pence was paid for each rat. In his book, 'A Sussex Life', Gilbert Sargent (1889 – 1982) recalls the activities of his local Club:

'You talk about cruelty today: well, I was brought up being cruel. When I was still going to school, we used to go out at night with clap-nets and lanterns round where the birds roosted. There used to be several thatched cottages about the place, and the old sparrows used to nest up under the eaves and we used to creep around and poke a stick up around the outside and out they'd come. We used to catch quite a lot of them; on average I suppose fifty or sixty different birds at night. We used to take them home and skin them. Well, we had to eat that because we didn't have anything for Sunday. I mean, meat! You just couldn't afford it. But birds, I've ate thousands of them: blackbirds and what we called greybirds, they were song thrushes. They'm jolly good, I tell you, you try 'em. Mother always used to make a pie of them. You skin them, you don't pluck them. Skin the breast off, because there's nothing on them really, only the breast. Then put a nice pastry top on and pop them in the oven. But you'd need a couple of dozen birds for a good meal . . . The number of birds caught must have run into thousands, and that was the cruelty of it. But people thought nothing of it in those days. It was a different way of life, not better or worse - just different. We used to go birdnesting all the time, taking blackbird and thrushes' eggs – moorhens' – all them. Brought them home and cooked them for tea.'

8. Upper Brickyard of the Marlpits 1887

Brickmaking probably started on the Forest in the sixteenth century. A survey of the Manor of Duddleswell, made in 1564, includes land called 'Le Brickefeilde' on the east side of what is now called Old Forge Lane and, although the traditional building material for the majority of houses and barns was wood up until the middle of the eighteenth century, the local ironworks required both bricks for lining the furnaces and tiles for roofing workshops and storehouses. The subsoil of the Forest provided suitable material for brickmaking almost anywhere, with more localised deposits of the finer-textured clay required for making tiles and there was plenty of brushwood for the faggots used to fire the kilns. Between Nutley village and the windmill, where a number of field names include the word 'brick', Richard Stevenson was said to have been working the lower brickyard as early as 1730, and members of the Stevenson family were involved in brickmaking in Nutley throughout the nineteenth century; in 1851 Benjamin Minns of the Shelley Arms was a tenant, supplying the capital for what was evidently quite a profitable business. By the 1870s, management of the Nutley brickyard was in the hands of a firm of builders, William Turner & Sons, and in 1887 William Turner junior became the owner of the premises and a second yard, known as the upper yard, was opened at Marlpits. This was the last one to operate in the parish of Maresfield, making clamp-fired bricks until about 1920.

9. Brickmakers at the Marlpits 1880

Before William Turner took over the Marlpits Brickyards they were run by the Stevensons, who not only made bricks, but manufactured tiles, pipes and clay pots, called 'crocks' and so they were known by the nickname of Crocker. In the photograph, farmer Laban Turk is standing to the right of the door with his wife and other workers at the yard.

10. Albert Turner's Timber Yard 1885

Albert Turner, son of William, owned a timber yard on Ford's Green which became one of the most successful local businesses. His father bought up most of the cottages in the village for his workers and at one time he owned one of the grocery shops and paid his workers in tokens which they had to spend there.

11. Mount Pleasant 1880

Mount Pleasant was situated at the bottom, forest end of what is now School Lane, where it joined the track leading up to the south side of the Crowborough, or Stonehill, Road. The lower Brickyard of the Marlpits lay to the left of the house and it is possible that the house was home to a local brickmaker.

12. The Sloop from Lampool 1890

The Sloop - or slope - is the stretch of the road between Nutley and Maresfield (now the A22), the road sloping down to a definite lower point and then up again to Lampool Corner where the old turnpike gates stood. This section of the road, together with the Straight Half Mile from Lampool Corner to Maresfield village, was built by Sir John Shelley of Maresfield Park with the proceeds of a Derby win. The two roads were contructed to keep the public traffic as far away as possible from his Maresfield estate.

  The road was set by surveyors with posts to line up the final surface measurement, the route straight and fairly even from Lampool to Nutley. However, the contractor, mindful of his costs and keen to keep infilling to a minimum, thus increasing his own profits, paid a boy to go at night and cut the tops off these posts. My grandfather, Herbert Kirby, heard this tale from the men who worked on Sir John's estate.

13. Pickett's Lane 1899

Pickett's, or Prickett's, Lane lies to the south of Nutley off the A22. The name has a variable origin for it could come from pricket, a young deer, or from pricker, a forester; if it is the latter then it might mean forester's entrance gate which sounds logical enough as Prickett's Hatch lies to the north-west, one of the forty gates or hatches in the medieval pale - a ditch and bank surmounted by a fence which allowed the deer to jump in but prevented them from jumping out of the 13,991 acres of Royal hunting forest enclosed in an early act of conservation by a thirteenth-century monarch. These gateways had an upper and lower division; the lower for persons walking on foot to go through, the upper to prevent deer from leaping over. Where these gateways existed long ago, the villages bearing their names can still be found: Friar's Gate to the north, Coleman's Hatch, Chelwood Gate to the west, Poundgate to the south. An old buckpen would stand near the gates, a kind of manger or trough made of oak on legs, where they would place food for the deer in winter.

My grandfather, Herbert Kirby, together with Great-Uncle George and Little Neddy Walter are shown here, planting larch trees on the left-hand side of the lane at the end of the last century. The trees survived until 1987 when, as recorded by Barbara Willard in her book, 'The Forest': 'On 16 October, in the small hours, there came that great wind that none of us who heard it will forget, blowing from the south with such violence and sheer ferocity that it grabbed all in its path, shaking and twisting and tossing. The roar of disaster increased as it travelled inland for ever unravelling what had been knitted by time, taking with it the landscape pattern of centuries. Ancient trees fell and their progeny with them, never to grow in the place they were destined to inherit. Tops were plucked off and hurled away like litter. Beech and oak, their roots a hundred, a hundred-and-fifty years in the making, screamed as they fell and at once began to die. In these few hours man was excluded, he was nothing; the battle was with older elements than intelligence . . .

The earth danced and spurted. At times, increasing the high fantasy, the moon emerged brilliant from flying cloud. A burning, salt-heavy atmosphere began at once to shrivel and destroy leaves already wilting . . . The word mammocked, that Shakespeare knew, seemed one to use when light came to show the Forest's face, twisted and distorted by this mightiest of strokes . . .'

The larch trees of Pickett's Lane were all felled by that great wind, the hurricane of October 1987 that destroyed great swathes of ancient woodland throughout the south of England.

14. Brook Farm Hop Gardens, Hole & Alchorne 1890

One of the hop gardens was on the Searles Estate which was owned by Sir Spencer Maryon-Wilson. Some fifty acres of land were cleared in the centre of Holly Bush Wood that lies between Nether Lane and Bell Lane and, being very labour intensive, the hopgardens provided employment for many local people. Every cottage stood empty in daylight hours, the schoolrooms deserted as men, women and children answered the call for unskilled labour. The sum paid was usually about 1/- for eight bushels, and the hops were dried in the two village oasts, one at Chantersell and one that became part of the old Memorial Hall. The workers wore hats to keep the sun from their faces, reflecting the nineteenth-century view that a skin burned by the sun was unbecoming, and indeed a misfortune in a woman.

Barbara Willard has a haunting tale of Forest behaviour told to her by a very old man of an incident he claimed to have witnessed as he worked with his mother in the Nutley hopfield: 'The story is of a young village girl with a baby born out of wedlock. She walked through the hopfield with the baby in her arms, and no-one glanced at her except my informant, who was then about eight years old. She moved slowly towards the nearby pond, which was deep. She stepped into the water and waded deeper and deeper. At last she vanished and the baby with her. "There was no hand raised to save her".' ('The Forest.')

15. Holly Bush Cottage 1890

Holly Bush Cottage was said to be haunted by the crying of a baby; it was the home of Thomas Carr and his wife Caroline, née Best, seen here in the doorway. A small bird cage hangs to one side of the door.

24

16. Granny Tester, Midwife 1905

There is some doubt as to whether this is a photograph of Granny Tester, and there is some confusion too about Granny herself, unless there were two redoubtable characters living but a few miles from each other at more or less the same time and bearing the same name. Nutley's Granny Tester was a midwife who lived on Ford's Green with a parrot and a young lad who had been badly burned, named Johnny, whom she had fostered. Sir Francis Champneys, Surgeon to Queen Victoria and Edward VII, who lived in the house now called Littlemead, had a very high opinion of Granny Tester's nursing and midwifery skills. He helped her with any difficult births in the village and thought she would have benefited from proper professional training in London, but the economics of the day did not allow for this, and she continued to serve the undoubtedly grateful womenfolk of Nutley.

Chelwood Gate's Granny Tester also had a reputation for good midwifery, and worked alongside her local doctor. According to this version, the doctor offered to help her go to London for training, but she could not leave her husband and eight children. She lived in a fifteenth century cottage in the Chelwood Gate area and although unable to read or write, was very smart over money matters and was an expert housekeeper for her large family. In the spring she and the children picked daffodils and primroses, bunching them for sale, and in the autumn they collected acorns to sell for pig food. It is said that she and her family would journey to her home village some six miles away to visit old friends and neighbours. Could this home village have been Nutley? Could these two ladies have been one and the same?

This photograph was recognised by some old Nutley people who swore that they 'would know her anywhere' despite the fact that she is not wearing her usual headcovering of a man's cap. Arthur Francis might well have substituted the cap for the shawl to make a better portrait.

17. Frank Divall, Mower 1898

Frank Divall was one of a band of professional mowers who worked locally cutting hay, corn or wheat according to the seasons, and who cut litter on the Forest for use on the large estates such as Maresfield Park, Sheffield Park, Hendall Farm and others. In 'Lark Rise to Candleford' Flora Thompson records that although the mechanical reaper was known in her childhood, it was looked upon as a farmer's toy; the scythe still did most of the work. 'The men still kept up the old country custom of choosing as their leader the tallest and most highly-skilled man amongst them, who was then called "King of the Mowers.". . . Every morning they set themselves to accomplish an amount of work in the day that they knew would tax all their powers till long after sunset. "Set yourself more than you can do, and you'll do it", was one of their maxims.' Perhaps Frank was Nutley's Mower King, with his scythe in his left hand, sharpener in the right and his leather gaiters, ready to work all hours of the day.

Frank Divall lived at Beach View on the Crowborough Road, so named because it was said that it was possible to see the beach at Pevensey from the upstairs window on a clear day. This photograph is thought to have been taken at Newbridge near the ford at the bottom of Kidd's Hill.

18. Aaron Scott, Turf Cutter 1890

Aaron Scott lived on the Forest all his life, much of it spent in a 'sod' hut near Spring Garden at Fairwarp, a dwelling made from a hole cut into a bank of earth over which poles and brushwood were laid, and the whole covered with growing turf. There must have been a number of these types of dwellings on the Forest; Thomas Pentecost wrote censoriously of Ashdown in 1852 as 'A healthy waste of huts and dens/Where human nature seldom mends . . .' Aaron was a turf cutter and used a breast plough for the job, similar to those used in medieval times. The removal of turf and peat from the Forest had caused so much damage that in 1830 it was agreed at a Commoners' meeting in the Maiden's Head Inn in Uckfield that 'poor industrious persons' would be allowed turf for fuel after applying for a ticket authorising how many turves at 1/- a load, an agreement which lasted another fifty-five years until 1885 when all turf and peat cutting became illegal. Clockhouse Lane in Nutley was once called Turfstack Lane, and there is still a Turfstack Cottage.

19. Ben Minns 1898

Ben Minns lived in Windmill Cottage by the old mill and styled himself an 'artisan hunter of Ashdown Forest ' – in other words a good old-fashioned poacher – and breeder of lurcher dogs. It used to be said of Nutley folk that they learned to set a wire – the poacher's snare – before they could walk, and anything that ran, swam or flew was a potential meal. According to Gilbert Sargent: 'Everybody used to poach in those days; all the old men did, but I was one of the biggest poachers when I was a youngster: catapults, snares, wiring rabbits, fish hooks . . . I could catch anything. I learnt a lot of my hunting and snaring from the old rabbit-catcher and I just sort of picked up the rest as I went along; if you're hungry it don't take long to figure out ways of catching things.' The old rabbit-catcher could have been Ben Minns who generously shared his skills with all the local youth, and Sargent recalls that 'some of the old foresters up around Nutley, they had some terrific dogs. One old boy had a lurcher called Trimmer, and my father used to have him up because the rabbits kept eating the flowers at Chapelwood. They was ferreting one day and

Trimmer was lying down aside the rabbit hole – we'd got the ferret down the hole and a rabbit popped its head up and the dog made a dive at it and the rabbit ducked back and old Benny Minns, he gave Trimmer such a belt and told him to stay. Then a couple of minutes later the rabbit jumped out and ran off and old Benny said, "Now's your bloody time!" and away he went and caught him too. Wonderful dog! He was a cross between a greyhound and an old English sheepdog.'

20. Dr. Fegan's Boys' Camp at Funnel's Farm 1908

Dr. Fegan was a philanthropist who lived in London and founded Fegan's Homes, the first being in Deptford, which aimed to provide a stable homely environment for orphans and children from deprived backgrounds. He held regular camps in the country similar to this one at Funnel's Farm in Down Street.

21. Crowborough Road 1885

The Crowborough Road takes the traveller from Nutley to Duddleswell across one of the loveliest parts of the Forest. Harry Walter remembers 'the road leading from Nutley when it was only about 9ft. wide. The road from Marlpits to Duddleswell was made about 1870, from Duddleswell to the Crowborough road was made in 1893, and before that there was only a forest track.' Nutley Windmill stands proud on the hill, Ben Minns's cottage clearly visible beside it; today the view is screened by trees. The farmer on the right, who could be Laban Turk, is unloading his tipper cart, using a mechanism which was both simple and ingenious: two pins would be pulled from the front of the cart, which would then pivot with the weight at the rear, and tip.

22. Ranger's Cottage 1910

This view of the Forest shows the old telephone exchange on the right at the top of the hill.

23. Jethro Senior and his son at Pippingford 1891

Jethro Senior and one of his sons are shown here harvesting on the Pippingford Estate using a sail binder. Canvas sails hung between the sweeps kept the corn clear of the cutting blades; the crop was then gathered, bound and stacked, or 'stooked' in a traditional form of husbandry that had survived from Roman times until the early years of the twentieth century. 'The corn was reaped, or later swapped by hand, and nearly all the corn was thrashed with the flail. All the grass was mown with the scythe . . . the work was all done by men, women and horses. All ploughing was done by horses and mostly with a turnwrist wooden plough; all very hard work for the men working on the farms of those days. The old men in my young days were nearly all very stooping, bent down by mowing, reaping and other heavy labour, as there was no machinery in those days to lighten their task, and their pay was 8/- a week. About 1840, Sir John Shelley acquired a hand-driven thrashing machine; four men turned winches to drive it; 15 minutes turning the winches and 15 minutes feeding the machine must have been very hard work.' (Harry Walter.)

24. Gypsy Caravans at Millbrook 1895

Gypsies were unwelcome visitors to the Forest, their presence a threat to Lord of the Manor and Commoner alike. Gilbert Sargent recalls stories of my grandfather: 'The Old Forest ranger, Herbert Kirby, he had to be a bit tough because it was his job to turn the diddies off the Forest. You got a lot of them at one time, the diddikais - gypsies - with their wheeled vans and horses. They'd pull up onto the Forest, and they was allowed to stay for so many hours to rest their horses and when their time was up old Kirby had to go and stir them off and they didn't allus take kindly to being moved along . . . sometimes the gypsies would get into fights with the village lads and they could be quite rough affairs, I tell you. I remember when I was first up in Nutley and working as a post boy, the old postmaster warned me about going past one of their camps, because when he was a bit younger he'd got into a terrible fight with some other blokes and a gang of gypsies up at the Shelley Arms at Nutley Fair, what they called Feast Day. They'd been drinking and several people got badly hurt.'

The curator of the Gypsy Museum in Selbourne, Hampshire has identified these travellers as the Harris family; the covered cart would contain fairground rides and the Harrises were operating small fairgrounds in the area around that time. They were probably travelling to the fairground in Nutley which had been established by Edward III on 27 July 1350 when he decreed 'that a fair be granted near the chapel of Notely in Queen Philippa's town of Maresfield on the eve and the day of St. George (22-23 April) during the Queen's life.' This was believed to have continued over the centuries until 1835 and held at Fair Place which is still known by that name.

25. The Harris Family at Fairplace 1895

26. Queen Victoria's Diamond Jubilee 1897

This towering bonfire, constructed on Ford's Green, was one of thousands built all over the country to celebrate Queen Victoria's 60 Glorious Years on 22 June 1897. The photograph suggests that the day was fine and warm, the umbrellas used in summer to protect the women as much from the sun as from the rain.

31

27. Nursery Lane 1888

In this carefully composed photograph, villagers in their Sunday best pose by a water garden in Nursery Lane; the apple trees of the orchard that gave the lane its name can be seen in the top right of the frame. Despite its artificiality, the picture preserves something of the unhurried pace of life in the 1880s; a sense of leisure and permanence that vanished forever after August 1914. Sitting on the bank to the right of the group is Owen Shoebridge. He was one of Nutley's postmen, and the son of Thomas, the village shoemaker whose speciality was 'a stout woman's shoe'. His brother, Tom, was the village schoolteacher, and his mother was a baker of excellent bread and kept a little shop. Harry Peckham recalls a most unusual gift: 'She had the reputation of being a charmer of warts, a gift which was hereditary in the family. The process was very simple; you took a piece of paper, went through the form of wrapping up the wart in it, and handed it to her and she took it without any incantations. But it was effectual in two cases of my own, one of a friend of mine, and one of a nurse maid. Certainly in the first three cases faith was wanting, for I only went through the performance for a joke and D. Westmacott (a friend, barrister and Civil Servant) wrote in a few days: "It's very odd, but my wart has gone". I had always heard that the best way to get rid of a wart was to steal a piece of raw meat and bury it, which is not an easy thing to do, as far as the stealing is concerned . . . Another way is to cut a cross on a stile on your way to church, and the next person to get over the style gets the wart; but I have no experience of this.'

28. Forest Gypsies 1890

The gypsies who made Ashdown their home were known as Forest gypsies, like this elderly couple pictured outside their bender, which was their shelter and their home. The bender was constructed on hazel rods, pushed firmly into the ground and then bent over to form a dome shape, which was then covered in canvas. The man is making a straw bee skep, or hive, by forcing lengths of straw through a short section of cowhorn and binding them together with bits of split bramble; this method of beekeeping was popular at the time. The woman is hanging a pot on a stout iron spike, known as a *kavvie saster,* to cook her food over the open fire.

29. Rod and Blanket Tent 1895

These Forest gypsies pose outside their rod and blanket tent, a simple cone structure, similar in design to the North American Indian tepee. The lower area to the left was contructed with a strong central ridgeboard, drilled at intervals into which arched hazel rods would be inserted. This was the sleeping area, around five foot high, which led into the living and cooking area at the front which rose to about ten feet. If the family was large, an additional sleeping quarter would be added to the opposite side of this. The whole wooden framework would be covered by blankets secured by long blackthorns, which had been fried in fat to make them pliable. The tent could be erected or dismantled within half an hour. Gypsy Wally Smith recalls stopping on the Forest: 'Sometimes we'd make a bender tent - take ten or twelve sticks about fifteen feet long, bend 'em over, put a cloth over the top - that's all we had to lay in if we never had a caravan. But the old coppers never 'ad no pity, even with snow on the ground and kids crying. "If you don't go, we'll tear your tent up" We never got no rest, no peace. If we sent the kids to school they come home and the caravan's gorn - moved on four or five miles.'

30. Ashdown Forest Temperance Band 1904

The Band was formed in 1902 and consisted mainly of musicians from Nutley and Fairwarp with a practice hut midway between the two villages. They provided a great deal of local entertainment until in 1911 when they split, 'by amicable decision', into two separate bands and 'the bandsmen formed up outside the band-hut and the two halves marched off playing in opposite directions, dividing into the Nutley Brass Band led by Charlie Wickham, and the Fairwarp Brass Band led by Ernie Best.' The Reverend Harry Peckham sits at the centre of the group, my grandfather, Herbert is seated behind the sailor.

I knew several of the musicians as old men and knew them not to be very temperate at all. They liked a 'drop of sherbert', sherbert being a generic term for all alcoholic drinks; 'going off to have a glass of sherbert' sounded less indulgent than having a glass of beer, although it fooled no-one. My father, Fred, recalls a story of the band: 'They was going to a fete at Fairwarp and the easiest way to get from Nutley to Fairwarp was through the Forest. Well, on the way through the Forest, one of these cornet players, 'e wanted to relieve hisself, so he laid his cornet down, and then when they got to the fete, he started blowing his cornet and he couldn't get no sound out of it, you see. So he pulled the tuning slide out of it, and when he'd laid it down, a little adder had crawled in that bell of the cornet and got down into that tuning slide. Yeh! It wouldn't have got into his mouth because it couldn't get up through the valves where you press them down, but when he see that adder come out . . . !'

31. Nutley Band on Feast Day July 1880

The third Friday in July was the date of the Feast Day for the Nutley Friendly Society; each member paid an annual subscription, out of which dinner and band were provided, and any remaining money was shared out on the feast day. The Society closed in 1909 because the fund intended for members in infirmity and old age had been dissipated over the years. Harry Walter recalls: 'The Club members assembled at the Inn about 11o'clock, each with a rosette of coloured ribbons pinned to his coat or smock frock; then with the two club flags at their head, marched with a brass band playing to the Church for a Service, and afterwards paraded Nutley street and back to the Club field (north of the Nutley Inn) to a meat dinner which was provided by the Publican. In the afternoon and evening both young and old village people enjoyed themselves. There were roundabouts, swings, boxing booths, shooting gallery, coconut shies etc., also stalls selling toys, ginger bread and whelk stalls; in fact, almost everything to take the eye and money of both young and old. The Band played dance tunes in the afternoon and evening, and the young women and men began the dancing and gaiety was in full swing until about half past ten. After that the field began to clear of the children and old folk, and after the bar in the Club booth had closed at 10 o'clock, where most of the men had been having a good time lifting glasses, many of the men were none too steady on their legs, but most of them thought they had been having a very good day, eating and drinking. Sometimes some got quarrelsome and ended up with fisticuffs. One feast day about 1775 I have been told there was a terrible fight between some rowdies and the gypsies, which ended up with several people getting hurt, but most Club days ended up with most people in very good humour.'

32. Black Ven Farmhouse, Nether Lane 1908

The name Black Ven is thought to be derived from black fen; there were a number of fen-like ponds in the area full of black water bubbling with marsh gases, caused by the peaty soil. The farm was part of the Searles Estate which was owned by Sir Spencer Maryon-Wilson who built his house entirely of stone taken from the Forest. The man at the gate is tenant farmer James Hobbs with, most likely, his second wife Susan; before Hobbs took it over, Walter Triggs was keeper on the Searles Estate and also Keeper of the Hounds at Black Ven Farm. In 1910 David Hobbs took over from his father and his tenancy continued until 1952 when the Searles Estate was split and Black Ven sold on. The Auctioneers description stated that the house had been divided into two parts, both very roomy, but with no mention of a bathroom in either, although water was laid on. There were then 55.531 acres to the farm and a number of outbuildings.

33. Black Ven Pond 1900

34. James Hobbs 1910

James Hobbs was born in Fletching in 1827, a fact confirmed by the Census of 1851 taken when he was 24. By that time his father, Edward was the tenant farmer at Chelwood Farm where he lived with his wife, two sons, a daughter and two agricultural labourers. The Census of 1861 shows that Edward had died leaving his widow, Emily, to run the farm. The couple's children, all unmarried, were still living with their mother. Another brother, Ernie, was reputed to have been killed in an explosion at the Powder Mills at Maresfield, and as he does not appear in either Census, he must have died before that time.

James moved on to farm at Spring Garden Farm at Fairwarp, and then to Black Ven around 1900. By this time he was elderly and had married twice. He passed Black Ven on to his son David in 1910, and died at the farm in 1924 aged 97. His long life spanned five reigns and he was witness to the rapid industrialism of Britain and the vast growth of national wealth, reflected in the imperialism of the late nineteenth century. The world he left would have been incomprehensible to the one he entered in 1827.

35. Jean Hobbs 1905

Jean Hobbs was the daughter of David and granddaughter of James Hobbs, of Black Ven Farm. When she grew up, she married Alfred Best and had two sons, William and Robert, who still live locally.

36. Nutley's Boy Soldiers 1902/3

On Lime Kiln Green in School Lane the village boys line up for imagined combat; on the left, Arthur Francis's son, Albert – the Company Commander – stands wearing his diagonal webbing belt and holding a wooden sword. Twelve years on these children would find themselves in the middle of a real war, where many Nutley men lost their lives; the War Memorial on the north wall of St James's church records the twenty names of those who fell. In the days of Napoleon, it was suggested by a noble lord that Sussex should send a regiment and that it would be a good thing to put the men of Ashdown Forest in the front line as they were full of the fighting spirit. This soldierly spirit undoubtedly was inculcated into the boys of the Forest too as an article from a 1922 issue of *Country Life* illustrates: 'About 1900 the boys of Nutley formed themselves into a Company and under their own officers armed with wooden swords of their own manufacture and other impedimenta of the battle arena, for years made mimic warfare . . . until with increasing age their enthusiasm carried them to such lengths that the battle's excitement got the better of discretion and blood flowed. It was then the juvenile soldiers had to be disbanded.' This was not before Albert Francis wrote to Field Marshal Lord Roberts in 1908 describing the Corps' efforts in making themselves into worthy combatants ready to serve their country, and requesting that they may be provided with a gun . . . This did not draw the reply they hoped for: 'Lord Roberts is very glad to hear you are learning drill at school but thinks you are hardly old enough to have a real gun yet.'

37. The Old William IV Public House 1913

The first William IV Public House in Nutley was an ale house situated at the southern end of the village a few yards off the main road to Uckfield. A very old property, it is shown on the Forest map of 1692, and was extended in the early 1800s to give more space for the bar. Fourth from the left is Fred Mitchell, Charlie Walter stands next to him in uniform. The landlord, Frank Blackman, stands in the doorway and the legendary mower, Dick Farmer, is on the far right. Gypsy horse sales were held at the old pub until 1920 when a new Public House was built a little further south. The new building took over from the old in 1928, and the old pub became a private house.

38. Nutley's Postmen 1896

Outside Whitewood Post Office and Grocery Shop, Nutley's postmen stand with the local policeman, PC Farley, and are, from left to right: Mr Streeter, Will Sayers, Will Wheatley, Owen Shoebridge, Arthur Sayers and John Tribe. Although two of the men are not in uniform, they were all officially employed by the Post Office and delivered the mail on foot and by bicycle. The longest-serving of these postmen was Will Sayers who joined the Post Office after leaving school on a wage of 3 shillings (15p) per week, and retired fifty-one years later, with a break during the First World War when he served in the South Staffords Regiment and was shot in the head on the St Quentin River in 1918 trying to wipe out a German machine gun post. The bullet proved impossible to remove, and doctors advised a quiet life, although I'm not sure whether postal delivery over rough terrain for the next thirty years was quite what they had in mind!

39. Will Wheatley, Postman 1890

Taken six years before the group photograph, a younger, rounder faced Will Wheatley was one of the best-known postman in the area. It was Will's job to collect the mail from Uckfield, some five miles away, with his own pony and cart for which he was paid 18 shillings (90p) per week by his employers to cover the cost of upkeep, stabling and feeding the pony, while he earned 12 shillings (60p) per week for this vital job. He married in 1913, a local girl born in Chelwood Common, just before being called up to fight in the First World War. A keen sportsman, Will played football and cricket for the village, and was a church bell-ringer.

40. Will Wheatley and the Post Cart 1890

41. Donkey Cart, High Street 1904

The people in this photograph are most probably members of the Greenfield family, who lived in the house shown in the background. Mr Greenfield was the village butcher and his house adjoined the shop which he ran until the 1914 war, when Bernard Grover took over the business. The shop closed in the 1950s and today it stands empty and derelict by the main road.

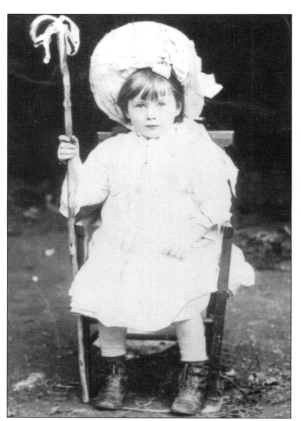

42. Etta Greenfield 1910

Etta, the youngest of the Greenfield children, was probably dressed up for the sitting, perhaps in the character of Little Bo Peep.

43. Butcher's Shop 1914

Bernard Grover's brother, Dick, stands in the doorway of the butcher's shop, a small but thriving business which served the growing community.

44 & 45. Frank 'Bicycle' Ridley 1911

Frank Ridley grew up at his father's farm in Old Forge Lane and had his bicycle shop in a number of different locations in the village. As his business grew and he needed more space, he built a shop opposite the church and branched out into motorcycles, then cars, and bought the old forge where he serviced and repaired cars and sold petrol. By the early 1900s, motoring was becoming universally popular; an act of 1896 had increased the speed limit to 14mph and done away with the earlier Highways Act which

insisted that all cars should travel at no more than 4mph and should be preceeded by a pedestrian waving a red warning flag.

By 1905, there were 15,800 private cars on the roads of Great Britain, although only three in Nutley belonging to Sir Spencer Maryon-Wilson, the Misses Cook and Sir Francis Champneys. In 1920 the Automobile Association opened its first roadside petrol filing station, the age of the car had arrived, and Bicycle Ridley was in position to take full advantage. The Ridleys owned the garage, and the modern petrol station opposite until the late 1980s.

46. Orpha Stevenson, Hop-Picker 1890

Orpha was born a Ridley on 15 June 1871 and lived in Chapelwood Cottages after her marriage. Seen here in the hop garden at Hole & Alchorne Farm in Bell Lane, she is collecting her hops in her umbrella, which, when empty, she would have used to protect her skin from the sun. The following extract from the parish magazine of October 1901 highlights the social and psychological benefits of hop-picking: 'Hop-picking has been the popular occupation during the past month. Many homes have been daily left without a single occupant. In vain the caller knocked or even tried the door handles; all portals were closed, and silence reigned within. Not even the voice of the baby could be heard, not even the venerable form of its grandmother could be seen about the premises, and the reason was that the babe in its perambulator, escorted by mother, grandmother, and every available member of the family had gone to join the picturesque and busy throngs who day by day gained health and vigour, and renewed youthfulness, and a little wealth, amidst the pleasant shady glades of the hop gardens. Certainly, judging by the improved appearance of many of the "pickers", the hop garden has a good claim to rank high amongst the more or less celebrated cures for human ailments.'

47. Alice Brown at Baker's Cottage 1885

Baker's Cottage lies just beyond the southern end of Ford's Green and was probably once part of Streatfield Farm. Owned by Benjamin Minns, it was tenanted by John Brown who died in 1866, leaving a wife and nine children. Left with no income, Mrs Brown started to bake bread in a back room, and sell it, together with meal and flour, to the villagers. There are records from 1877 of her trade, and she must have done very well because in 1893 she bought the cottage and the land on which the first Nutley Telephone Exchange was built. She died three years later, leaving her two unmarried daughters, Phyllis and Alice, to carry on the business, which they did for the next twenty years, baking twice a day and delivering the loaves in big baskets covered in white cloths.

48. Mrs Grey of Pippingford 1890

Pippingford – or Pippingworth – Park first came into being under the Decree of 1693 when a specially appointed commission decided that of the 13,991 acres of medieval hunting forest, 6,400 acres would be left for the use of the Commoners and the remaining land enclosed. This followed a lawsuit brought by the *Earl of Dorset & his Lessees versus John Newnham & Other Commoners* in 1689 which was to change the face of the Forest forever. The champion of the Commoners, one John Newnham of Nutley Inn, pleaded at law for the rights of the Commoners, so long threatened by the vagaries of authority, to be upheld against the Earl and others whose efforts to enclose and develop the wild heathland were continually thwarted by 'the crossness of the neighbourhood'. The court found in favour of the Earl, and the map of Ashdown was redrawn, the new enclosures lying within the original pale now beyond the reach of those Commoners who had set out their claims so boldly. Pippingford had been enclosed some thirty years before the Decree by William Newnham, who lived at Maresfield Park, and this enclosure, along with Old Lodge, became the largest award with 2,175 acres; since when it has had many owners and uses including ironworking. In the early nineteenth century, the estate was acquired by William Bradford who built the first mansion, and it was during the course of a wedding reception in 1836 that the house caught fire – tradition tells of an overturned oil lamp, a drunken butler . . . Unfortunately the date was November the 5th and those who saw the smoke and flames concluded that Mr Bradford and his friends were enjoying a Guy Fawkes celebration. Under a new owner, a wealthy Mr Mortimer, the house was rebuilt in 1857 in the style of a French chateau under the direction of architect Hector Horeau, then at the height of his fame: an original drawing made by the architect was exhibited in London in 1859 with the caption, *Castle recently erected in Sussex*. After Mortimer's death in 1871, the property passed to Mr Grey, who is believed to have been his nephew and reputed to have been a pleasant man and well liked locally, but judging by the great age of Mrs Grey, seen here with her black groom and pet dog, it wouldn't be long before Pippingford changed hands again. Captain Banbury of the Royal Engineers became the squire during the first years of this century. He frequently invited his military colleagues to conduct summer exercises over his land, and it was partly because of this that the Army moved in quickly to already familiar territory in 1914. When, after considerable occupation of those war years, the Forest returned to civilian life, the connection remained, and does so to this day. The land is used by the MoD as a training area, but the estate is now run with nature conservation as a prime objective. As there is no public access, the wildlife which is driven out of much of the Forest proper by continual public intrusion finds sanctuary in the wild tranquillity of this tract of land in the centre of the Forest.

49. Pippingford Park 1890

50. Old Lodge 1910

Old Lodge lies above the shallow valley known as Old Lodge Bottom and has the appearance of a Tudor manor house although this facade is misleading as it was added by the De La Warr family around the turn of the century. Harry Peckham recalls being told about a team of phantom horses who walked some distance beside one of his parishioners one fine moonlight night near Old Lodge, although whether alcohol had a part in this he doesn't reveal.

There were six medieval Walks of the Forest, each with a lodge constructed of wattle and daub within a wooden frame, set on shallow foundations and thatched with heather, strategically placed to command views of the walks and facilitate control of game and poachers, which exposed position led to rapid deterioration and the need for regular repair. A warrant of 9 July, 1524, authorised the Duchy of Lancaster to pay Sir Thomas Boleyn (father of Anne) £27 for the expenses he had incurred in making five new Forest lodges, and although it does not name them, it is possible that one of them was Old Lodge; one of the cottages on the dependent farm dates back to Tudor times. In John Hatton's Survey of 1632, carried out for Charles I with a view to the sale of the Forest, the six lodges of the Forest were reported in poor condition.

51. Charcoal Burners at Masketts 1890

The charcoal-burner has tales to tell.
He lives in the Forest,
Alone in the Forest;
He sits in the Forest,
Alone in the Forest
And the sun comes slanting between the trees . . .
And he sits and thinks of the things they know
He and the Forest, alone together –
The springs that come and the summers that go,
Autumn dew on bracken and heather,
The drip of the Forest beneath the snow . . .
All the things they have seen,
All the things they have heard:
An April sky swept clean and the song of a bird . . .
Oh, the charcoal-burner has tales to tell!
And he lives in the Forest and knows us well.
A.A. Milne 'Now We Are Six'

Two charcoal burners at Masketts Farm are seen here building a charcoal clamp, an elaborate structure which took great skill and patience, for the outer casing had to be almost a complete seal, while allowing just enough air in to maintain the fierce fire within: 'They'd build up a dome of cord-wood, billets about three feet long. Then when it was all built, with a chimney-hole down the middle, they'd cover the whole thing with litter - straw and such like - and then cover with wet sand and turf. Then they used to put some burning charcoal in at the top of the chimney and put a plug of turf on top and then just let it slowly burn right through the stack. Sometimes it took a couple of days; they knew when it was ready by the colour of the flame that came out of the top. Then they'd pour water down inside and when it had cooled off, they'd rake all the turf and litter off and you've got your charcoal. The wood looked just the same as when it went in, right down to the knot holes, except it was charcoal. They used charcoal for all sorts of things: gunpowder, shoe-blacking, hop-drying . . .' (Gilbert Sargent). The men slept on site in benders, ready to attend the constant needs of the fires which burned on through the night. One local tale tells of two men, father and son, who slept while fumes seeped from a faulty clamp into their shelter, and both were found dead in the morning.

47

52. Nutley's Fire Engine 1910

The Fire Engine did not belong to the village at all, but was owned by Sir Stuart Samuel who built a house at Chelwood Vachery in 1907 on the site popularly thought to have contained the medieval hunting lodge of Edward II. Foundations of an ancient building were still discernable in 1856 and when the Reverend Edward Turner of Maresfield, founder of the Sussex Archaelogical Society, reported that he had found a silver coin of Edward II on the site, he declared this was irrefutable evidence. The name Vachery first appears in 1292 in the surname of one Nicholas ater Vachery, the name held to derive from vacherie, a dairy farm. Sir Stuart built an imposing house with gables, chimneys and a central tower, which enjoys wide views of the Downs. In order to protect the property and surrounding woodlands from fire, he employed the services of this horse-drawn fire engine, with the aptly named Mr Sparkes as driver; he was also the local scoutmaster and was known as Gandhi, although whether because of his moustache or opinions or because Sir Stuart's brother was Viceroy of India, no-one is quite certain.

53. Edwin Russell 1880

Harry Peckham writes of Edwin Russell: 'He was a harmless imbecile, said to have relations very well off, but they never took any notice of him. He was said to have been brought up by his grandmother till one Sunday being left at home to watch the cooking of the dinner, he took up the kitten and popped it alive into the pot in which the dinner was boiling, and fled. And from that time forwards he lived a wandering life in the villages around Nutley; although no-one would admit him into their house, most people were ready to give him bits to eat, or boil his kettle for him. He used to wear a top hat generally trimmed with feathers or coloured paper; he had medals stuck about his coat, and was pleased with any sort of bright coloured decoration. He carried a kettle which contained his worldly goods, and he had an old accordian with which he used to make a noise. He used to say that only fools and donkeys worked and he never lowered himself to that level, but he and I were good friends and I used to give him baccy; but I fancy he did not smoke but only chewed . . . He used to sleep anywhere; once he laid for weeks in an empty pigsty which he made so filthy that its owner turned him out. One man told me he would not have cleaned it out, no, not for a shilling. Another time he slept in Jimmy Tester's wheelbarrow which stood in an open shed, just four posts and a roof; but he was ousted from there because he would sing in the night to the accompaniment of his accordian. I have been told that he used to take off his clothes and pile them on his head. One winter's morning after a very white frost, I was down on Dodds Bottom when a woman told me old Edwin was dead, lying under a hedge; I went there and there he lay covered with rime. I prodded him with my stick and up he jumped, asked for baccy, and shambled off. During one of those hard winters in the '90s, he got frost-bitten and lost some of his toes, so we sent him down to the Infirmary at the Workhouse (in Uckfield) where he spent the winter very contentedly, and took his discharge in the spring to resume his old wandering life. After that we used to catch him every year as the weather got cold and send him down to what he used to call "the fatting coop". He died before I left Nutley, and was buried at Fairwarp, to the surprise of most people as, if he had a settlement anywhere, it was at Nutley. I believe he was a good deal over 70, so his outdoor life had not hurt him.'

54. Boringwheel Mill, 1880

Down at the southern end of the Forest, on a headwater of the River Ouse, lies a large lake known as Boringwheel, one of the evocative place names that recall the once-powerful national iron industry that was centred around Ashdown. When the historian William Camden (1551-1623) visited the Weald, he found it 'full of iron mines in sundry places, furnaces on every side . . . to which purpose diverse brooks in many places are brought to runne in one channell, and sundry meadows turned into pooles and water, that they might bee of power sufficient to drive hammer milles'; in the deep Forest valleys, rivers and streams were dammed to provide the considerable water power needed to turn the wheels of mills grinding corn or to drive the blast furnace bellows in the forges.

A grain mill at Boringwheel was converted to bore out the barrels of the iron cannons that were cast locally, a tradition that continued until the 1770s. When the local iron industry declined, the mill reverted to grain, and in the latter part of the nineteenth century was run by a Mr Simmonds in partnership with William Taylor, the miller at Nutley Windmill, who worked a sensible division of the elements. When there was plenty of wind, or the water flow was low, the windmill was used. When the water ran high and fast, or there was no wind, the water mill was brought into action. The windmill ceased to operate in 1908 when William Taylor retired, but the watermill ran for some years after that before it was closed.

55. Chantersell Farm 1890

The name Chantersell is a corruption of Chantry Sale, or land sold by the church, and this land is thought to have belonged to an old church said to have stood in the High Street where Nutley Hall now stands. Very old foundations were discovered there by builders and recorded by Harry Walter while the Hall was being built at the turn of the century.

On the left of the photograph, two men are engaged in the practice of goose cramming, or force feeding, while the women on the right are plucking chickens. The scene looks over Holly Bush Wood towards Fletching.

56. Gypsy Camp, Crowborough Road 1895

This camp site was situated on a triangle of manorial waste adjoining the 150 acres of the Nutley Inn Farm (now Nutlin Fruit Farm) and was a traditional stopping place for local gypsies. The photograph shows a traditional Reading van on the left and what appears to be an old railway carriage on the right. These were often converted by gypsies for travelling on the road.

57. Nutley Windmill 1890

Nutley Windmill is a unique survivor of a type of open trestle post mill first seen in this country 800 years ago. According to local tradition, it came originally from Goudhurst in Kent – a mill had disappeared from the village in the mid 1700s – and having stood for some time in Crowborough, arrived on its site by Stonehill off the Crowborough Road in the mid 1830s. Henry Setford is said to have been the first miller, and then it passed through several hands until William Taylor, who lived at Tudor Cottage in the High Street, took it on and ran it in partnership with Mr Simmonds, owner of the Boringwheel watermill in Cackle Street, and between them they made full use of wind and water power. It was a working mill until William Taylor's retirement in 1908, when it closed down and became almost derelict. The windmill became the property of the Earl and Countess Castle Stewart when they came to live at Old Lodge in the 1920s, and in 1968 permission to restore the mill was given to Tony Turner, founder of the Uckfield and District Preservation Society. In five years the mill was back to full working order, earning for the Society a European Architectural Heritage Award; since then a continuous programme of maintenance and renewal has enabled the mill to be opened to the public on a regular basis.

58. Stonehill to Camp Hill 1890

The old English name for an enclosed area is camp or comp and, as early as 1564, the Duchy of Lancaster lists *Campysshill* in its records, and a boundary bank nearby could be the remains of a sixteenth century enclosure. Two centuries later, its name might have suggested it for the site of a military camp which was struck on the Forest in the summer of 1793, when war with France was in its early stages.

In 'A Shropshire Lad', A.E. Housman recalls a similar camp:

> On the idle hill of summer,
> Sleepy with the flow of streams,
> Far I hear the steady drummer
> Drumming like a noise in dreams.
>
> Far and near and low and louder
> On the roads of earth go by,
> Dear to friends and food for powder,
> Soldiers marching, all to die.
>
> East and west on fields forgotten
> Bleach the bones of comrades slain,
> Lovely lads and dead and rotten;
> None that go return again.
>
> Far the calling bugles hollo,
> High the screaming fife replies,
> Gay the files of scarlet follow:
> Woman bore me, I will rise.

Records show that the encampment, which covered ground from Duddleswell to Nutley with lines of tents, kitchens, trenches dug for exercises, and various administrative sections, held a force of 7,000 men, including horse and foot who, under the command of the Duke of Richmond, assembled on the Forest to test the efficiency of a new drill system introduced by General Dundas before they moved on to Brighton where they drilled for a fortnight before the Prince of Wales. Mystery mounds in the area, which had excited archaeologists for many years, were revealed as recently as 1964 to be the field kitchens for the militia; in the Museum at Worthing, a lady's fan commemorative of three 1793 camps, one being Ashdown, is decorated with a stylised plan of each.

59. Forest Enclosures 1880

The enclosure seen to the right of the photograph, and another that is just out of the left of the picture, were made by two of Tinker Wright's sons on the Forest below the Lower Brickyard of the Marlpits before the Enclosures Act of 1886. They are now known as Ardens and Little Birches. Three children in the foreground on the right of the photograph can be seen collecting litter in their handcart.

The wooden enclosure halfway up the track probably surrounded a forest spring from which water would be drawn and carried home in two buckets hung on a yoke over the shoulders, a practice which continued on the Forest until well after the Second World War.

60. Charlie Catt's Bus 1905

Charlie Catt farmed the 150 acres of Nutley Inn Farm and ran a bus service between the village and Uckfield, doing a round trip twice a day in the summer months, once a day in winter. The bus was built for him by his father-in-law who, as well as being an expert carpenter, worked on the land as a sheep-shearer and cowman, driving and working eight oxen when he was a young man. The bus, with its red plush interior upholstered by Charlie's wife, was always kept in immaculate condition, the horses had coats 'like polished ebony' and the harnesses and brasses gleamed. The driver wore a hard hat and a coat with a velvet collar, and flourished a long whip which was purely for show as the horses knew the stops well and pulled up of their own accord if they saw a passenger waiting. This first bus was replaced by a larger one, drawn by several horses and carrying twenty people, with those on top needing an umbrella in wet weather. The photograph shows Charlie Catt riding with the driver, with Harry May the blacksmith posing by the bus and some of Charlie's 10 children standing at the back.

61. Horse Artillery at Marlpits 1907

On a site previously used for intensive clay digging, the horse artillery trains for war. Sweet Minepits cottage can be seen in the background.

62. Bell Lane 1908

Bell Lane took its name from an old inn, The Bell, which stood at the Nutley end of the lane which runs from Fletching village. Forest stone was used for road building, and it is possible that this steam roller had run into trouble while flattening the stone to make good a road surface near the Searles Estate. Alf Grover, brother of Bernard, stands to the right of the photograph, a log over his shoulder – perhaps to lever the steam roller out of the ditch, or to feed to the traction engine to work up an extra head of steam to pull the stricken vehicle out.

63. Village Wedding 1912

The marriage of Lena Turner of Nutley to Dr Inman of Fairwarp took place in 1912. Lena was the daughter of Albert Turner, owner of the brickyard, the timber yard, various farms and a number of residential properties, and the man who gave the village its first village hall, known affectionately as the Albert Hall, which stood on the High Street at the junction with Nether Lane. The marriage of his daughter would have been an important social event for the village.

64. Holly Cottage 1913

Holly Cottage was built by Nelson Turner on a plot of land encroached before the Act of 1886. For many years it was occupied by the Walters who brought up a large family there and were virtually self-sufficient, growing vegetables and keeping poultry, and using their Commoners' rights to graze a pig and cow on the Forest.

65. Jasper Wickham 1890

Jasper Wickham lived in one of the two cottages belonging to the Turner/Ridley family of The Orchard, Nether Lane, and he shared his home with his wife, son Charlie and Charlie's wife and children. The two cottages are now one dwelling, and the only survivor of the old estate which made way for a development of new houses in the 1980s. It is thought that Jasper worked for the Turner family which is why he lived in the property, and this photograph was taken in the cart shed that stood on the triangle of land at the junction of Nether Lane and the High Street, with a twitten forming the third side. Charlie started up Nutley's own Brass Band from the remnants of the Ashdown Forest Temperance Band and became its Bandmaster.

66. The Vicar's Tea Party 1913

Charles Neill succeeded Harry Peckham as the Vicar of Nutley in 1913 and his youthful looks may account for all this attention from the women of the village for an unrecorded but undoubtedly rather smart occasion in the gardens of the Vicarage, now a private house called Forest Mead.

67. Nutley Football Team 1890

Nutley's football team of 1890 comprised:

Back row from left to right: Mr Schrubb, Frank Farmer, Tom Diplock, Edward Gorringe, Tom Appleby, Mr Carr, Gerald Mead.

Middle row: Will Riley, Albert Turner Junior, Frank Whitewood.

Front row: Graham Taylor, Owen Shoebridge.

68. Nutley Cricket Team 1908

Members of the 1908 cricket team includes Albert Turner Junior standing fourth from the left in the back row, Will Weller and Walter Coleman seated first and second from the left, Herbert Appleby holding the trophy with Ted Gillham seated on his left. The Reverend Harry Peckham stands to the left of the group, next to umpire George Kenward, the village undertaker, whose workshop was behind the butcher's shop. The other umpire is John Taylor.

69. Stoolball on Ford's Green 1896

Stoolball was a popular game, a precursor of cricket and once played all over the country with a paddle bat which defended a small rectangular shoulder-high wooden goal. The game was played on Ford's Green; the trees around the Green were planted that year.

70. Little Nurse 1914

This portrait of an unknown child by Arthur Francis has an added poignancy in view of the date.

71. Artists' Rifles on Ford's Green 1906

The Artists' Rifles were raised in 1859 by Lord Leighton, President of the Royal Academy; part of the City and County Regiment of London which had twenty-eight battalions, the Artists being No. 28, they were formed from the Middlesex Volunteer Rifles by members of the artistic community – painters, writers and artists. Their badge was of two heads, Mars, the god of war, and Minerva, goddess of the arts, both wearing helmets, the latter with a snake emerging from it; this badge was usually made of white metal, but occasionally appeared in blackened brass. In 1937 they joined the Rifle Brigade, returning to Maresfield during the war as an officer cadet training unit; ten years later they became the 21st Battalion of the S.A.S.

Posing on the southerly side of Ford's Green in 1906, the future for these soldiers is an unknown country, but on a summer day in 1906 the world seems secure and permanent. The one-storey building to the left is the old Mission Hall, demolished at the end of the 1950s; the cottages on the right are still there.

72. Harry Walter 1915

Harry Walter was born in Nutley on 6 March 1872. His father kept a cow and other animals which young Harry helped to tend when he came home from school, and when his schooldays were over, he went to work on the Forest digging stone and gravel for 2 shillings and 4 pence per yard (about 12p). In 1891 he started work at Woodlands Nursery for thirteen shillings per week for a 63 hour week, but his real love was carpentry, and in 1896 he started his own wheelwright and carpentry business, sometimes subcontracting to Mr Gillham and other local builders. In 1903 he built his own workshop where he worked until the war broke out, when he became the wheelwright at Maresfield Park. After the war, he started working for H. & E. Waters, Builders of Forest Row, and worked, among others, on Chailey Heritage's Operating Theatre, High Beeches Convent and the Macmillan property at Birch Grove, before becoming self-employed again. His memoirs, in the form of vivid diaries which recorded his Forest childhood and the conditions he faced as a working man at the turn of the century, have been drawn on heavily for this book. The originals are now kept in the Public Records Office in Lewes.

Harry made this beautiful cart for butcher Bernard Grover, a man keen on good workmanship and careful with his money. The cart was treated with three coats of paint, each coat being carefully rubbed down before the next was applied. Harry was paid £12 for the cart, to include all the materials, and reckoned he made ½p per hour out of the contract.

73. Harry Walter's Model Sussex Wagon 1916

Harry, seen here on the right, made this model Sussex wagon which was to be filled with rosebuds from the gardens of Nutley and taken to London for a presentation to Queen Mary on St George's Day. It was known to have been in the British Museum up until the Second World War. Walter Biles, headmaster of the school, stands beside him.

74. Forest Hall Chapel Members 1903

Forest Hall Baptist Chapel was opened in 1897 and lies to the south of the village on the Forest edge. It is still in use, and this photograph was taken on Good Friday, 1903, to commemorate the chapel's sixth anniversary.

Back row, left to right: George Tunks, David Curd, Robert Avis, Albert Walter, George Kenward.
Middle Row: William Hall, Phyllis Brown, Hester Walter, Mrs Avis, Lizzie Avis,
    Mrs May, Mr May.
Front row: Hannah Best, Mary-Ann Gander, two Scottish girls, possibly Lena and
    Jessie, Mr Moorcock, Mrs Moorcock, Mrs Tunks, Emma Walter.

75 & 76. Nutley Inn 1912

Nutley Inn was a fine old Georgian coaching inn built about 1807 by Squire Newnham of Maresfield Park and it was an important staging post for travellers on their way to the coast from London; a stopping place for drovers taking their sheep to high pasture on the Downs in the summer months. On a sunny day in 1912, the schoolchildren have gathered outside the Inn for some occasion which, judging by the elaborate cars and top-hatted attendant, could have been a wedding and might have been the marriage of Lena Turner to Dr Inman of Fairwarp which was a grand village affair and took place in the same year (see plate 63).

The suspended penny farthing bicycle and the double porches on the front of the Inn disappeared when it became the Shelley Arms in 1919. The pond opposite the Inn can be seen clearly in plate 76.

77. Coppice Cutting 1900

Areas of woodland, known as cants, were rented out and the wood harvested for domestic and commercial purposes. Whole families would work together on their cant, cutting hazel for pea and bean sticks, and birch poles to make wooden toys; sheep hurdles and wattles were manufactured from chestnut. It was an excellent way of managing woodland, keeping it clean and productive, and in the last few years a coppicing programme has been restarted by the Forest Conservators to cut hazel in Cackle Street, alder off Kidd's Hill and sweet chestnut in an area by the Ridge Road.

78. Ford's Bank 1890

Ford's Bank drops steeply off the ridge which carries the A22 south of the village, opposite Ford's Green, which one old map has as Wickers Green, but it remains Ford's, or Foord's in all other records. This view was used by Whitewoods as a postcard, Number 113 in their Photo Series, and shows three cottages built by Nelson Turner on land encroached before the Act of 1886. The cottage in the distance was built on the site of Tinker Wright's hut (see plate 5), today known as Lavender Cottage; Holly Cottage is on the left and on the right is Ranger's Cottage.

79. Shoeing an Awkward Horse 1890

The horse involved in this complicated shoeing had a reputation for kicking, so an ingenious frame was designed and set up by blacksmith, Harry May, to avoid injury. He stands well back on the left, leaving the job to his apprentice, while the owner of the 'ockerd oss' stands on the right. The forge was on the site of what became Bicycle Ridley's premises, and eventually a car showroom.

80. The Three Gables Stores 1912

The Three Gables Stores (the third gable is behind the creeper) served as a village shop for many years, and was used by the Whitewoods before their new shop, the Post Office and general store, was built across the road in the 1860s. In 1912 John Thorne was the owner and to judge from the advertising hoardings and cluttered window display, it was a well-stocked shop. The old stone and brick structure was demolished during the 1980s, and the five modern houses built on the site retained three gable ends and the name of the old store.

81. Land Army of The First World War 1914

A mobile unit of the Women's National Land Service Corps (WNLSC) was officially formed by the government in 1916, but the women in this photograph predate that foundation by two years. The 1914 post mark is clear on the verso of this postcard, sent by a Nutley correspondent to a friend in Brighton; the writing is indistinct and gives no clues as to location, although it could be the Nutley Inn Farm which became the Nutlin Fruit Farm. The women are undoubtedly posing for this photograph, using their tools and produce as props, and to judge by the large pile of clay pots in the foreground, it must have been in a large market garden or farm. This volunteer force was drawn both from town and countrywomen who were predominantly middle class and therefore able to work for nothing, having private means or the support of their families. They were trained in many trades, including those of carters and milkers, and there were two local training farms at Fletching and Danehill. Their uniform consisted of strong boots over leggings and corduroy breeches, shirts or smocks worn with a tie, topped by a large soft hat, a new departure for women who, up until that time, were unused to wearing trousers in public.

82. The Tylers, Whitehouse Farm 1882

The Tylers were first recorded at Whitehouse Farm in Horney Common in the 1800s when John Tyler, a shoemaker, married Sarah Willis, last surviving daughter of Thomas Willis, owner of the Farm and the last forgeman at Old Forge. Sarah inherited the farm and John developed the Willis family business of corn chandlering, carting and selling cord wood into a traditional grocery business which he ran in conjunction with his own shoemaking trade. His son, Jacob, ran the farm, and his grandson Enoch, seen here with his family in 1882, took over the farm and the grocery business, and the family also made bricks at a site near the top of the lane which now bears their name. Enoch's son, Allan (second from left) opened Tyler's Stores on the main road opposite the gate to Horney Common – which was at one time a gate to Maresfield Park – and both farm and shop were run by him until after his death when his son, Cecil, sold up in the mid 1950s. The shop continued for another twenty years, before becoming a private house, and the new owners of Whitehouse Farm renamed it Jades Farm, although the original name was transferred to a nearby house, and still exists today. Standing with their father are, from left to right: Sally, George and Mabel, Allen and Luther. Enoch's wife Ann, sits with baby Lizzie in her arms.

83. Whitehouse Farm 1890

84. Enoch and Lizzie Tyler c1900

Enoch is photographed with his youngest child, Lizzie, who died a few years later in her early twenties.

85 & 86. Nutley School c1900

The site of Nutley school was given to the village by the Earl and Countess De La Warr on 22 April 1853, shortly after the church and ecclesiastical parish came into being. No records are available of the date when the school was built, or opened, and it is not until a year after the Education Act of 1870 which made education compulsory for all children up to the age of twelve, when Miss H. Reed was in charge, that the first records began:

Extracts from the Log Book:

1871 Nov 30th. Mary Jane Harris appointed sweeper at a payment of 3d. per hour.

1872 Jan 12th. Mary Jane Harris left school.

May 3rd. There were 135 children present (Miss Reed appears to have worked with only monitors to help her).

May 10th. A new classroom opened.

1874 Sept 21st. Only 40 children present; the rest away gleaning, hop-picking and collecting acorns.

1877 Jan 12th.	Mr H. Coleby in charge. Mr Thomas Shoebridge started as Pupil Teacher. The number on the roll was now 145, the only accommodation 2 rooms (now rated as sufficient for 97) so it is not surprising to find that children outside the parish are taken off the roll.
Aug 23rd.	Attendance this week the highest this quarter, probably owing to the school treat.
1882	The infants' room added at the end of this year.
1887	Four children suffering from 'glass-pock'.
1893	Mr H. Adams in charge.
1897	
Feb 1st - 18th.	Free soup provided.

The school at this time became a family affair. Mrs Adams and two daughters were also on the staff.

| 1901 | Mr Walter Biles in charge. |
| 1911 | The West Room added. |

Harry Peckham had much to do with the running of the school in its early days. Responsible for the appointment of good teachers, he didn't always get it right: '(Mr Leeke) answered my advertisement for a married man; and when he discovered he was likely to get the appointment, he wired an offer of marriage to a lady of his acquaintance, and unfortunately for him she accepted the offer; for she was an untidy, lazy woman. Leeke was not a bad master, and an excellent low comedian for which nature evidently intended him, to judge from his face. But both he and his wife were bad managers. He told me, in the course of one of his periodical applications for an advance of salary, that when he married he had not a £5 note and had no idea how much he owed; and at last he got so hopelessly into debt that the village tradesmen stopped supplies, and he had to go.' Peckham's tolerence was further stretched when sickness struck the school; he might have been refering to 'glass-pock' when he wrote: 'A very trying time for the Correspondent was when the third Plague of Egypt was prevalent, in a very virulent form described as "they body ones". Mothers used to come to me weeping or raging, and asking who was to pay for the changes they had to burn. I suggested that boiling would save the necessity of destroying, but was told that was impossible in the case of flannel. We found the plague proceeded from one family, and we told the parents that the children would not be admitted without a certificate that they were free and their house disinfected; we refused them admission when they came, and the Attendance Committee prosecuted them for non-attendance. Thus we drove them out of the neighbourhood, and the plague was stayed.'

In view of this unchristian attitude, it is not surprising that for many Victorian children, school was an unwelcome official interruption of their daily routine; most children played a part in the family economy, and there was so much to learn which could never be taught in books: stone-picking, bird-scaring, collecting wood, haymaking, bean and pea-setting being only a few of the jobs undertaken by Sussex village children listed in a report of 1867. Some of their elders remained sceptical as to the value of education for all, as expressed by old Captain Vye in Thomas Hardy's 'Return of the Native' : 'There's too much of that sending to school in these days! It only does harm. Every gatepost and barn door you come to is sure to have some bad word or other chalked upon it by the young rascals; a woman can hardly pass for shame sometimes.'

By the age of thirteen, the children were ready to leave. A Labour Certificate would be issued to prove that he or she had reached a certain level of education (or school attendance for at least 250 days during the past five years was also accepted as proof of competence) and the children would go out into the world to make their mark: in trade, onto the land or into service in one of the big houses.

87. Nutley Schoolchildren 1878

Harry Walter attended the school when this early photograph was taken:

'In my schooldays, 1877–1882, there was a schoolmaster named Colby, a very strict master. One of the teachers was a man I liked very much as a teacher, Mr Thomas Shoebridge. I remember once, with three other boys, being kept in for being backward at lessons. The Clergyman came in and asked the schoolmaster why. He said we were three duffers! I made progress from then onward.'

Tom Shoebridge, brother of Owen, stands in the middle of the back row. He kept scrapbooks of newspaper cuttings of local events from 1870 to the 1900s which I have drawn on for this book. Graham Taylor, a trainee teacher, is on the left of the second row from the back. Graham never left the school he attended as a pupil, taking on the post as trainee straight from the classroom at the age of 14.

88. The Boys of Nutley School 1915

At the turn of the century, Nutley was an isolated community with limited access to the world outside. Families tended to be large, intermarriage was common, and a number of names dominated the voting register: Wickham, Ridley, Walter, Turner, Scott, Stevenson. When there are several, sometimes dozens, of people with the same name within a contained community, the use of nicknames becomes common practice as a means of identification, hence Tinker Wright, Crocker Stevenson, Bicycle Ridley. In the village today, a nickname is still a matter of great pride and a symbol of belonging.

Back row, left to right: Leslie Stevens, Greasy Wickham, Adge Bishops, Fred Penfold, Fred Kirby, Ted Turner.

Middle Row: Fred Harding, Frank Stevenson, Eddy Wheatland, Charlie Streeter, Ernie Stevenson, Frank Baldock, Victor Wickham, Charlie Ridley.

Front row: Ted Blackman, Bert Mitchell, Ron Bishops, Leonard Parkes, Joe Ridley, Jasper Wickham (my godfather), Charlie Wickham.

89. The Girls of Nutley School 1915

Back row, left to right: Evelyn Powell, Lissie Stevenson, Esther Tester, Kathy Savage, Dolly
                                Ridley, Dolly Hazeldene, Laura Ridley, Alice Taylor.
Middle row: Kathy Walter, Bessie Davis, Ivy Walter, Maud Kirby, Gladys Scott, Rose
                                Walter, Unknown, Amy Marchant.
Front row: Dolly Carr, Lily Ridley, Ethel Ridley, Dorothy Mitchell, Nellie Jupp,
                                Kitty Penfold, Chrissie Wickham.

Fairwarp

Apart from Nutley, Fairwarp is the only other village on the Forest, a rather modern place which seems to have grown from a single farmhouse built in 1777 on a track across the Forest; there is no trace of it or the road that runs through it on the Ordnance Survey Map of 1805, although by the 1880s it was a growing community with a church and school, post office and pub. However, the name is referred to as early as 1519 when, at the 'Coorte holden at Notlye' on 10 October, among the many complaints made to the King's officers by the people of the district was that 'all the byrche wood between Notlye and Fayre Wharpe hathe bene felede.' Thirty loads of timber had been taken, 'to the grete hurte of the Kynge and his tenantese', and disposed of at Lewes and other places by the rangers.

J. Heywood Horsburgh writes extravagantly to his 'Dear Friends' from the Fairwarp Vicarage in 1906: 'Last summer I was abroad amidst some of Nature's grandest and most famous scenery. This summer – well, I am at Fairwarp! A contrast? Yes. Nevertheless England has a special beauty and grandeur all her own; and this romantic little village bears its witness to the fact. The view from Duddleswell: the wide stretching moor clad in loveliest heather; the fresh wind blowing up from the sea; the restful solitude without loneliness; the welcome quiet without stagnation; the general peacefulness of all; the sunny grasslands, the shady woods; the hills and the dales; the delightful feeling of expanse and freedom – all these, and more, must impress the Englishman who visits Fairwarp with the unique beauties of his own dear country . . .'

When the Romans annexed Britain, Ashdown was part of a much larger forest they called Anderida. They pushed through their great road from London to the port in Lewes, passing over high ground by Camp Hill and Duddleswell, laying the foundations with slag and cinder from the ancient iron workings found in the area. The road, built around AD 100, was only discovered from air photographs taken in 1929 by Ivan Margery, author of 'Roman Ways in the Weald', who traced its course where it enters the Forest at Chuck Hatch and rises to King's Standing, passing north of Beggars' Bush and east by Streeter's Farm (the name here may mean 'Dweller by the Street') before dropping down through Fairwarp, skirting the ironworks at Oldlands, and leaving by Lampool to continue straight and true to Malling Down east of Lewes.

> The Roman Road runs straight and bare
> As the pale parting-line in hair
> Across the heath. And thoughtful men
> Contrast its days of Now and Then,
> And delve, and measure, and compare;
> Visioning on the vacant air
> Helmed legionaries, who proudly rear
> The Eagle, as they pace again
>   The Roman Road
>   *Thomas Hardy*

90. Bracken Road Clump, Duddleswell 1900

This is the view from King's Standing across to Bracken Road Clump, now known as the Crow's Nest, and beyond to the long line of the South Downs. In 1816 a meeting of Commoners held at Nutley decided to mark certain stretches of ground, known as reservations, with wooden posts, 10 yards apart. It was agreed that no litter – bracken, heather and gorse – would be cut in these reservations and they would be used for the rearing of blackcock and pheasant. The five reservations were at King's Standing, Gill's Lap, Five Hundred Acres, Crow's Nest and Hollies Down. The wooden posts soon rotted and the Lord of the Manor succeeded in establishing the clumps of Scots Pine which were planted as landmarks.

In the foreground, the Commoners' cattle grazed in safety: 'Nearly everybody who had a small plot of grass on their holding, within the Forest pale, used to make a small stack of hay for winter feed, kept at least one cow and sometimes two, as well as a young bullock or two, according to the size of their holding, but relied on the Forest for grazing for their stock practically all year round, as did most of the farmers for summer grazing, and also turned out their farm horses when farm work was slack. Pritchetts Hatch Farm horses were turned on the Forest most weekends, and the young bullocks from Funnells Farm were turned out to graze all the summer months and they used to employ a lad to tend them. I have seen as many as 60 head of young stock and cows belonging to other smallholders crossing Ford's Green to the Forest for grazing.' (Harry Walter).

91. Old Lodge Road 1904

92. Oldlands Hall 1890

There is evidence to suggest that iron was smelted from the rich ore of the Weald long before the Romans came, and they were quick to realise the potential of these iron workings - for use in London or for export to the Empire - and extended the industry, notably at Oldlands, where a number of Roman coins from the reigns of Nero (54-68), Vespasian (68-79) and Diolectian (284-286) have been found. Iron production at this time was a skilled hand operation by small groups of men mining the ore, cutting and burning wood for charcoal, and operating the furnaces. The name, said to mean the 'old ironworking lands' of Roman times, appears as 'Eldelond' in an old document of 1219 and was the traditional name of the valley and land now covered by Oldlands Wood; the industry had declined after the Romans and was not revived until the thirteenth century and places known to have been worked by the Romans came to be called 'the old lands', 'the old forge' to distinguish them from the new centres being opened up. The industry really began to flourish from the end of the fifteenth century and iron brought to Ashdown its greatest prosperity, and also its greatest physical change. From dense forest, 'thick and inaccessible, a retreat for large herds of deer and swine . . . wolves and wild boars' recorded by the Venerable Bede in his great book 'A History of the English Church & People' in AD 731, it became Cobbett's 'most villainously ugly spot' as the forests were denuded. Charcoal fuelled the furnaces, vast quantities of timber were swallowed up and soon there was an outcry about the enormous proliferation of iron mills in the south-east; the fear was that there would be no wood left to build houses and ships. The industry reached its peak at the time of the Spanish Armada when arms, and particularly cannon, found their way to ships of both sides . . . The poet Michael Drayton had much to say against those who cut down Sussex timber for their furnaces:

> These forests, as I say, the daughters of the Weald
> That in their heavy breasts had long their grief concealed,
> Foreseeing their decay each hour so fast come on,
> Under the axe's stroke, fetched many a grievous groan:
> When as the anvil's weight, and hammer's dreadful sound,
> Even rent the hollow woods and shook the squeachy ground.

In 1896 the Reverend J.L. Ward Petley, Curate of Maresfield, writes:
'It is not easy for us to picture our quiet and rural Sussex the busy centre of our country's iron works, yet such was the case. Two hundred years ago there were in Sussex 42 forges and 27 furnaces with all their blast and smoke and dirt and noise in full swing. And no unimportant part did they play in our country's history. The iron guns and iron cannon balls of old Sussex gave a good account of themselves on many a hard fought field, and eventful battle both by sea and land. The first iron cannon made in England was cast by Ralph Hogge, at Buxted, in 1543 in the reign of Henry VIII. His home, The Hog House, still stands, opposite the school . . . It was Sussex guns and Sussex shot that helped to drive away the Spanish Armada from our shores. Foreign countries also sought shot for guns from Sussex ironworks, that in 1572 laws had to be passed to stop their exportation "less the enemies' ships be too well armed . . .". Not only were our shot and guns greatly prized and readily sold, but other iron work too. Richly decorated and quaintly designed fire backs and irons with fire dogs, were much thought of . . . iron was put to more uses than it is now. Milestones were made of iron; iron slabs did duty as tombstones.'

> Noise of hammers once I heard
> Many hammers, busy hammers,
> Beating, shaping, night and day,
> Shaping, beating dust and clay.
> *Ralph Hodgson*

In 1866 the Oldlands estate was sold to the poet Coventry Patmore who built a house on the site of a medieval farmhouse and used various different names over the next few years: Buxted Hall, Oldlands House, and finally Heron's Ghyll when he sold the land to Alexander Nesbitt who in 1870 started to build the present Victorian mansion, called Oldlands Hall. Later the Hall became home to a Spanish grandee - Bonaventura Paula Misa, a sherry merchant, and was then sold to a South African magnate, Sir Frederick Eckstein, whose son, Bernard, constructed the huge iron entrance gates. Sir Bernard lived there until his death in 1948 when Oldlands Hall was sold to a Hove builder for £30,000 and converted into flats.

93. Oldlands Farm 1900

Oldlands Farm is a sixteenth-century ironmaster's house, built on the Oldlands estate and connected with the later Tudor furnace. Near the farm is an old ice-house, hewn out of solid sandstone, in which meat and game would have been stored. Ice taken from the nearby lake in winter would have remained solid for several months and kept the food fresh. In 1841 the farm was owned by Benjamin Minns, a local landowner, who lived there with his wife Mary and son John. Ten years later they were still there, farming 80 acres and employing two workers. By 1861, Benjamin had died and his son John had taken over who lived there with his wife, also Mary, and their two sons, Albert aged 2 and Benjamin eleven months. The latter became a well-known 'artisan hunter of Ashdown Forest' and lived at Windmill Cottage (see plate 19).

94. Old Forge looking towards Cackle Street 1900

According to Harry Walter: 'The Old Forge near Fairwarp made horseshoes for King Edward in his war against King Bruce of Scotland, and a lot of the railing around Old St. Paul's were made at Old Forge which was being worked as late as 1827. An old man told me he could remember hearing the hammer at work when he was a boy. The last Ironmaster was named Willis. Boringwheel Mill was reputed to be first used, not as a corn mill, but for boring out the inside of cast iron guns that were cast in the forges in the neighbourhood. There were many traces of small smelting places on the Forest where a small forge was set up, used for a while and then abandoned, perhaps for want of iron ore or wood for smelting.'

Reminders of this once great industry are all about the Forest: Furnace Wood, Cinderbank, Hammerpond, Old Forge Lane are some of the names that evoke the past; slag and cinder fragments can be found in banks and streams, forest streams are stained by iron compounds. Industrial clamour interrupted visions of a forest bright with birdsong:

'A great deal of meadow ground is turned into ponds and pools for the driving of mills by the flashes which beating with hammers upon the iron, fill the neighbourhood round about night and day with continual noise' contains a report written in 1722. By the nineteenth century the industry had removed itself to other parts of the country where coal was the favoured fuel, and time has healed that ugly blackened expanse that Cobbett writes of in such disgust.

95. Ashdown Forest School 1890

The school, always referred to as the Forest school, was opened in 1873 as an infant's department for the Maresfield parish school. In 1890 there were 64 children on the register; by 1906 that number had risen to 198. The attendance register for that year records some familiar names: Cottingham, Horscroft, Hazelden, Walter, Tester, Osborne, Hobbs, Tunks and Dadswell among them. Gilbert Sargent attended a similar church school elsewhere in the county: 'I was about three or four when I started school. It was about half a mile away from the cottage up by the church, and I stayed there until I was twelve; then I had to leave and get a job. We had two rooms, a large one for the bigger kids and a small one for the infants. We had long desks so you sat in rows and scratched away on old slates – spat on them to clean them. But for all that, we learned absolutely nothing really: a bit of reading and writing, and what they called object lessons, where we'd have pictures of objects like animals or household things or perhaps food. We'd have to recognise them and know about them.'

> Object Lesson 1892/3
> *Animals: cow, elephant, sheep, horse, tiger, lion, dog, cat*
> *Food: bread, butter, sugar, cheese, rice*
> *Trades: tailor, baker, farmer*
> *Minerals: coal, iron, glass*
> *Clothing: calico, flannel, silk*
> *Phenomena of nature: rain, sun, spring, summer*

The Parish Magazine of 1906 congratulates the head, Mrs Burgess, on receiving one of the best reports the school has ever received from the new religious inspector and quotes his report: 'I was much pleased with the work of the school. The infants answered well and seemed interested in their works. In the upper divisions the repetition and Catechism were said very well and the majority of the children gave intelligent and correct answers in the Old and New Testament subjects, although some did not seem to exert their thinking powers . . .' School meals were introduced nationally that year because of concern over the number of recruits to the Boer War suffering from malnutrition.

96. Christ Church 1895

Christ Church was designed by Rhode Hawkins in the early English style and consecrated by the Bishop of Chichester in November 1881. Built of local stone on a site beside the school at a cost of £2,000, it consisted of a nave, chancel and vestry, with no spire or tower but a small turret at the west end containing two bells, and was served by the rector of Maresfield and his curate. The east windows were a memorial to Alexander Nesbitt of Oldlands, and the west windows commemorated Elphinstone Barchard of Duddleswell. Other gifts included a brass lectern in the shape of an eagle, a font and pulpit made of marble and stone, and a genuine Della Robbia brought back from Italy by Miss Hermione Eckstein, which hangs in the wall of the side Chapel. In 1901 Fairwarp became an independent ecclesiastical parish within the civil parish of Maresfield, and had its own vicar, the Reverend G.C. Pimbury. In 1935, the east end of the Church was completely transformed when Sir Bernard Eckstein, of Oldlands, erected the present tower and chancel in memory of his father, Sir Frederick; its unusual design reflected Sir Bernard's wish that it should be modelled on that of Pretoria Cathedral in South Africa, to commemorate the fact that his family had business interests there, as can be seen on the bronze reliefs on the family tomb in the churchyard. The surrounding fir trees were spared, on the wishes of local inhabitants, to soften the unexpected outline of the tower in the Sussex countryside.

97. Heron's Ghyll 1900

In 1866 Coventry Patmore, poet and Catholic convert, became owner of the Oldlands estate and with it bought a large farmhouse of medieval origin called Pucksty, the name meaning pixie's or fairy's field, from a Mr Benham, a man of sinister reputation who kept a mistress in Minns Cottage and had caused the death of his wife in such dreadful circumstances that her ghost was said to walk the drive.

Patmore built a new house, described in a *Country Life* of 1903 as 'cast in the early Tudor mould, with a fine domestic character, foreign to all that is merely cold and stately in its features, and with gardens all appropriate to the time, sweet in its reticence and quietness, fragrant in its floral richness, true in its spirit of enclosure . . . Indeed there is everything here to please the most critical in architectural matters, the whole of the buildings, both in character and details, being in most excellent style. It has its quaint leaded panes between excellently moulded mullions and transoms, finely worked walls of stone, good gables and chimneys, all domestic and attractive. Such houses are in many places in England, both old and new . . .' The poet left Heron's Ghyll in 1874, having sold the Oldlands estate to Alexander Nesbitt, and in 1879 the house was bought by the Duke of Norfolk for the Dowager Duchess Mina who built a school and established a Catholic mission there. Her grandson, James Fitzalan Hope, later Lord Rankeillour, built the Catholic church of St John the Evangelist in 1897 in the early English style and bought Stroods and Barnsgate to extend his lands to over 10,000 acres. His own initials and his wife's can be seen on either side of the wide archway to the left of the house, the Hope coat of arms is over the front door and the crest over the fireplace in the great hall dates back to 1896. He remained in the parish until the house was leased to Temple Grove School in 1935.

98. Duddleswell Stores 1914

An old forester, Bill Coleman, recalls the store: 'Well, at Fairwarp, you could get practically everything you wanted. Shoes, boots, coal, chicken food – there wasn't anything you couldn't go in and get. A bale of hay, everything was there except bread. Now bread used to come round with a horse and cart from Buxted, round about three or four times a week. Milk - Mr Cottingham, down at Lampool Corner, you know the oast house there? He'd come round with the old horse and cart and take it out of the churn, a pint or half-pint, he used to pay you a visit every morning.'

99. Fairwarp Farm 1910

It is possible that an old house on the site of Fairwarp Farm might have been the original dwelling around which the village grew after 1777.

100 & 101. Fairwarp Club Day 1906

The Parish Magazine of June 1906 contains the following report: 'On Wednesday 13th the event of the year for the people known as Club Day, took place. The day's programme opened as usual with a Service in the Church, there was a fine congregation present, including about one hundred members of the Friendly Society, whose voices were heard to great advantage in the hearty singing of our popular hymns "Onward Christian Soldiers", "Oh God our help in ages past". An address was given by the Vicar from Rom. xii 2. Immediately after the service a procession was formed up outside the Church gates and headed by the Vicar, the Secretary, and Mr E. Kenward marched into the village in time to the enlivening strains of our local Brass Band. Here in a large tent a splendid dinner was served by Mr Osborne. After the usual Royal toasts had been given and responded to, the Vicar proposed the toast of the day. After congratulating the members on belonging to such an excellent Club, he spoke a word of praise for its financial position which considering the time it had been started, stood better than any Club in the neighbourhood; although there was a considerable drain on its resources last year through sickness, its funds for the year showed an increase of about £30 and its reserve fund now amounts to £808 17s 2d.'

102. New Pond Cottages from the Crow's Nest 1898

With a powerful magnifying glass, it is possible to see a horse and cart, loaded high with litter, in the right hand foreground of this photograph; possibly the same cart shown in close-up in plate 103. 'In my young days men living in and around the Forest used to get a good part of their living working on the Forest. From leaving school I went to work on the Forest with my father, and all through my teens litter cutting, stone and gravel digging; very hard work for very little money. In those days we used to dig gravel and stone for 2s 4d a yard. After the first of August people, both men and women, used to cut and sell bracken to farmers and to Woodland's Nursery. They used about 80 waggon loads a year. Sir Spencer Wilson (of Searles) had possibly 100 loads of brakes and litter each year, and farmers and stock keepers at Barkham, Newick and Fletching had many loads for their cattle bedding. Then there were loads of turf and peat cut and carried to houses around the neighbourhood for house-firing; none used now, we now buy coal at 5/- a hundredweight. Turf used to cost 12/- a waggon load delivered, enough to last a cottage's house fires all the winter.' (Harry Walter.)

103. Litter Cutting 1898

Brake fern or bracken was cut with a 'swop' or sickle while still green; litter was the term used for all the vegetation that fell to the scythe – mainly bracken, heather, furze or gorse, broom and coarse grass, which was cut later in the autumn when the heathland had turned a rich russet shade just before the first frosts. Local farmers valued it as a cheap and effective substitute for straw, and used it for overwintering their stock before putting it onto their fields.

This photograph is taken just to the right of the little ghyll or stream which runs down from below King's Standing to New Pond Cottages, and can be seen quite clearly in plate 102.

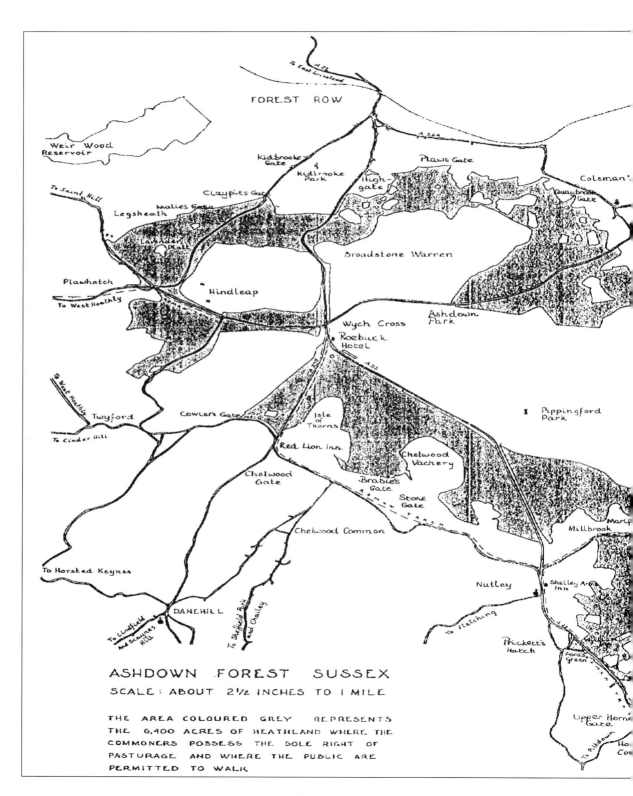

ASHDOWN FOREST SUSSEX

SCALE: ABOUT 2½ INCHES TO 1 MILE

THE AREA COLOURED GREY REPRESENTS
THE 6,400 ACRES OF HEATHLAND WHERE THE
COMMONERS POSSESS THE SOLE RIGHT OF
PASTURAGE AND WHERE THE PUBLIC ARE
PERMITTED TO WALK

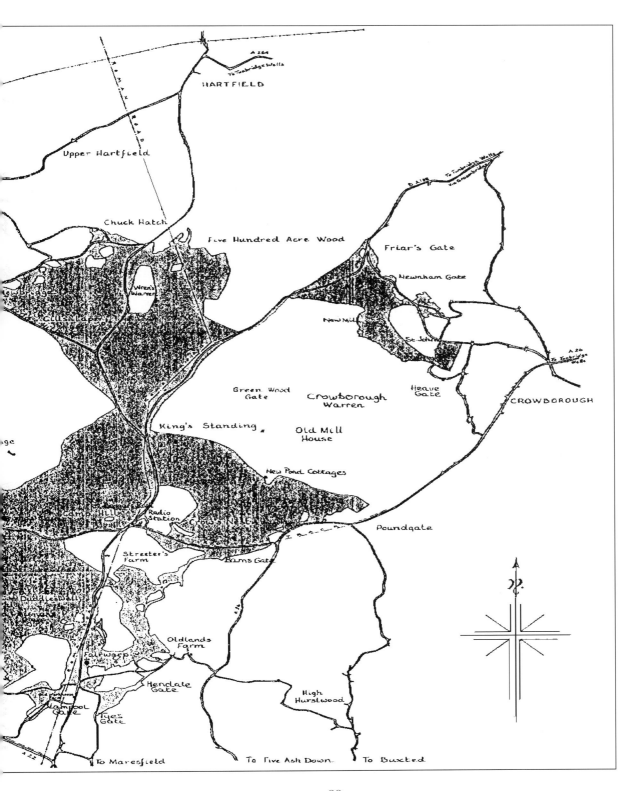

HARTFIELD

Upper Hartfield

Chuck Hatch

Five Hundred Acre Wood

Friar's Gate

Newnham Gate

Wren's Warren

New Mill

St. John's

Green Wood Gate

Crowborough Warren

Heave Gate

CROWBOROUGH

King's Standing

Old Mill House

New Pond Cottages

Radio Station

Poundgate

Streeter's Farm

Brins Gate

Oldlands Farm

Fairwasp

Hendale Gate

High Hurstwood

Nanpool Gate

Tyes Gate

To Maresfield

To Five Ash Down

To Buxted

104. Nursery Lane and Woodlands 1890

'An industry which flourished for nearly a century between Fairwarp and Maresfield was Woodlands Nursery. The founder of the business was a Mr William Wood who, after the Napoleonic war was over, bought a small farm there and started a nursery (in 1824). He used to tell his workmen he followed both the allied army and the French armies as well, as a trader in hardware goods, and traded news as well to each. He hired many acres of land (120) from Sir John Shelley and at one time it was the largest nursery in England with the outlying farms of Spring Garden and Copthall as well . . . At the age of 19 I started work at the Woodlands Nursery and when I asked for the job, Mr Wood told me to bring my working clothes with me. That was what they told everyone in those days, 1891. I worked there until I married in 1892 when they raised my pay to 13/- in the winter and in the summer to 14/- for a week of 63 hours. When I got home on Saturday nights, the cupboard was mostly empty and I had to go to the shop before we could have our tea. The shops were kept open till 10 o'clock on Saturday nights, as we did not get our wages till Saturday night in those days . . . Woodlands passed to his son Mr Charles Wood who used to employ at least 60-70 men and boys in the winter months during the planting and taking up period. The nursery contained many thousands of young fruit trees of every sort and kind; all known species of conifers and bush and standard roses, acres of them. Besides greenhouse plants, heathers and flowering shrubs, rhododendrons etc. Men from Fairwarp, Maresfield and other places used to find work there; in the summer they trained the peach, nectarine, plum and cherry trees some time before it was time to begin taking it up for sale. The orders were lifted carefully, packed and sent by waggon to Uckfield station, and the waggons generally came home loaded with London manure from the railway. The nursery carried on until about 1918, but gradually declined after the death of Mr Charles Wood, and the remaining stocks of trees and plants sold by auction.' (Harry Walter.) There was an ale house in Nursery Lane and the drunks would crawl into the woods just to the right of this photograph which became known locally as Slut's Hole, until Lady Shelley of Maresfield Park renamed it Nightingale Wood!

105. Spring Garden Farm 1894

'I have been told the land of Spring Garden Farm was encroached from the Forest by a man named Gilbert. He is buried in Maresfield Churchyard, and on his tombstone is carved a pick and shovel. His grave is one the south side of the belfry. I have heard he was a smuggler as well as a farmer; some years before when a wall was knocked out to make alterations at the Farm, several bottles of smuggled spirits were found. His house and the house at Lower Misbourne Farm were both built to the same plan.' (Harry Walter.)

Whether or not he was a smuggler, farmers were known to be helpful; Durrant-Cooper, writing in the Sussex Archaeological Collections in 1885 says: 'It was the custom of farmers to favour the smugglers so far as to allow the gates in the fields to be left unlocked at night; and to broach without scruple the half-anker of Schiedam (gin), which was considerately left in some hayrick or outhouse.' The wives of farmers often put out bread and meat on the gates for the men, and on all the smugglers' routes there were houses, cottages, farmhouses and inns where cargoes could be hidden in secret rooms, cellars and barns. Many were so well hidden that they were forgotten; Harry Walter recalls a man finding a bottle of proof spirits in the mud while clearing out a spring, and he records a tale told to him by an old man he worked with a Woodlands Nursery:

'He told me his father used to work in the winter thrashing corn with a flail. In Hendal Barn a farmer came to him and asked him to have one bay cleared; the next morning when he went to work, there were a lot of kegs of spirit covered up with straw. He had not worked long the next day when a farmer from a neighbouring farm came in the barn and asked him, after sniffing about, where it was, and he told him under the straw. He then pulled out a gimlet, bored a hole in one of the kegs and had a drink, then plugged up the hole. Three or four times that day, farmers and gentry came to the barn and did the same. The next morning the kegs were all gone, but one very small keg left for him and a note, to say nothing of what he had seen . . .'

106. Faggot Cutting 1890

Wood cutting in the winter gave employment to a number of men and many of the farms had a certain amount of woodland which would be cut on a wage basis for the farmer, or bought outright in cants. When the coppice was ten or twelve years old, it would be cut and sorted out into house faggots – that is bundles of brushwood containing a certain number of 'bats' and fastened by benders, into lordlings – longer brushwood and suitable for use as pea boughs, and chestnut saplings, the best used for hop and bean poles, the remainder for fencing and wattle- making. Every house had its faggot stack, used to fire everything from the hearth to the old copper pots used for laundry; two waggon loads of forest turf and two hundred faggots represented the average quantity of fuel used by a cottager each year.

107. Oldlands Miniature Rifle Club 1906

A report from the Parish magazine records: 'Quite an important ceremony took place in our parish on Wednesday, the 4th of July, when the new covered Rifle Range was opened. It is situated in one of the Oldland's fields, within easy reach of the village, and so will be very convenient for all parishioners wishing to join in. For this most generous gift we have to thank Mr Misa of Oldlands Hall, who has presented the range and had it erected at his own expense. It was hoped that Lord Roberts would have been able to come and perform the opening ceremony, but owing to his many engagements he was unable to do so, however, we had the next best thing, his nephew, Major Maxwell. This officer, after addressing a few manly words to the members on the subject of rifle ranges and their object according to Lord Robert's theory, then fired the first shot and declared the range opened. Just before leaving with his party, the Vicar proposed a vote of

thanks for Mr Misa for his generous gift to the neighbourhood, and also thanked Major Maxwell for his trouble in coming to open the Range. This was followed by a public Tea given by Mr & Mrs Misa at which upwards of one hundred took advantage. The Brass Band was present and played at intervals. The Range will be opened every Thursday . . . We cannot speak too highly of Mr Misa's project, it will not only help to amuse our young men in their spare moments, but also train them to be good shots and perhaps, some day, useful defenders of their country . . .'

108. The Osbornes of the Foresters' Arms 1900

Originally a private house, The Foresters' Arms' first recorded licensee was a James Cordeux in 1882. William Osborne took over in 1898 and remained there for the next thirty years, during which time he and Mrs Osborne, seen here with four of their nine daughters, brought up eleven children. The pub was at the centre of village life, a meeting place for all the local societies and clubs, and some rather more bizarre gatherings: 'On the evening of 13 July Henry Padgham was found dead in his garden. He had not been seen since morning. At the Inquest held at the Foresters' Arms, an apoplectic fit was put forward as the cause of death. Deceased had just been pensioned off, after many years service with Lord Sheffield as coachman. Having bought Cinderbank Farm, he was getting the house in order to receive a bride when the sudden call came. Such is life!'

109. Three Sisters 1905

Clara, Sophia and Minnie Osborne.

110. Toll Farm 1912

Toll Farm stands at the Fairwarp end of Cackle Street on what could have been an old toll road, or the name could have come from the Sussex dialect 'towl' meaning a clump of trees. The possible derivation for the name of the lane could be that a cockle was a seventeenth century term for a hop-drying kiln.

111. Woodcutters 1910

Two woodcutters have flawed, or stripped, the bark from an oak tree and stacked it on the trunk of another tree to dry. The bark would be cut into small squares with a hatching tool, and then bagged and sent to a local tanyard; there was one in Maresfield, also Buxted, Danehill and Edenbridge. When the empty sacks were returned, they usually contained some leather with which the men soled their boots. The bark of oak, willow, birch, spruce and chestnut was put in a tanpit, or vat, with the hides and the process took a year to complete. After use, the tan was sold as manure, or made into cakes and burnt as fuel. The poles in the photograph have been cut for use in the local hop fields to support the hop binds, or vines.

112. 'Ammy the Axe' 1914

The axe is one of the oldest of human tools, and the skills involved in its use little changed since the Stone Age. 'Ammy the Axe's' real name was Fred Weller, a Fairwarp woodsman who felled Forest trees with an axe and crosscut saw.

113. The Gorringes of Brown's Brook 1906

Brown's Brook appears as Brown Brook on a 1795 Fadon's 1-inch map of Sussex, and that may be its true name; the water is often brown. On the other hand, there is a mention of a Brown's Lodge - and therefore presumably a Mr Brown - in a 1540 report of a commission appointed to enquire into waste of timber and destruction of game on the Forest, and a 1564 complete survey of the Forest mentions Brown's Brook. The hut Charlie Gorringe and his wife (pictured here) lived in had three rooms, two with earth floors and one with brick. Their son, also Charlie, was blinded in a shooting accident at the age of sixteen, but he made a living making baskets and mats and became an accomplished fiddle and mandolin player.

114. The Temperance Band 1903

An early photograph of the Temperance Band, taken before they were issued with uniforms (see plate 30), Bicycle Ridley is second on the right. Nutley's musicians disbanded in the late 1920s, when a number of the players rejoined the Fairwarp Band which carried on playing until 1971. By that time the older musicians had died and interest in the Band died with them. Some of them had played with the Band for over thirty years, including Alfred Walter, a regular at The Foresters' Arms, who started with the cornet and ended up playing a double bass horn.

115. The Ashdown Forest School Cricket Team 1910

116. The Ashdown Forest School Stoolball Team 1910

117. The Village 1906

There was enormous rivalry between the villages of Nutley and Fairwarp: 'they was always at war; didn't matter what it was over - any old thing, such as a football match or cricket match, they'd often end up in a pitched battle. Like at Christmas time, the Forest always had plenty of holly on it and there used to be fighting over that, because they used to cut it by the cartload and ship it up to Covent Garden and make quite a bit of money out of it.' (Gilbert Sargent).) That much of it was also friendly is evidenced in the surnames on the registers of the two village schools.

The village was home to a number of colourful characters: 'There was a man living at Fairwarp who was supposed to be a wizard and people used to go to him to have their fortunes told, and if their cattle strayed or were stolen he was supposed to tell them where they were. Many tales have been handed down about him. One tale is, he was thrashing corn in Nutley Inn barn and the servant maid hid his dinner bag; he found it but told her he would pay her out before next day. When she went to bed she could not undress or lie down; she had to walk her room till morning. He asked her next day how she slept the night before; she played no more tricks. Another tale was, someone tried to steal his grindstone, got it on his back but could not get out of the garden or get the grindstone off his back, till in the morning the old man looked out of his bedroom window and told the would-be thief he could now take it off his back and go home.' (Harry Walter.) Dame Garson from Duddleswell was a famous nineteenth-century witch who was said to adopt the shape of a fox or hare; the local hunt invariably ended up outside her cottage where the hunted animal would disappear through an open window before she appeared to ask the huntsmen if they'd had good sport.

118. Ginny, Alf and Baby Allitt 1904

Alf Allitt farmed at Boringwheel Mill for many years, and married farmer's daughter, Ginny Penfold, seen here with their eldest son, Alfred. Every year Alf provided the horse and cart to transport the village children from the Forest school to and from the train station at Uckfield on their annual outing to Brighton.

119. Binding the Oats 1912

Alf Allitt working the land at Boringwheel Mill Farm, cuttings oats with a binder with his three-in-hand.

120. Spinners 1910

121. Camp Hill, Duddleswell 1904

Duddleswell, an old name meaning Dudel's or Dudeney's spring, was one of the six medieval Walks of the Forest, and a Royal Manor. There is a St Dudeney's chapel marked on an early ordnance map, and in 1855 the remains of a large old building, thought to be ecclesiastical, were unearthed by a tenant farmer.

A collection of small farms and isolated houses, Duddleswell was also thought to be the site of a Roman posting station, the remains of which were uncovered during the construction of a radio station on land requisitioned by the government during the last war, but which, in the urgency of the time, had to be covered and forgotten. The present nineteenth-century Manor house stands opposite the site of a much older house, and by the Duddleswell crossroads stand three yew trees; traditionally these trees marked those farms ready to overnight drovers and their animals, the old Drift Road runs nearby and Streeter's Farm is conveniently at hand.

This isolated community was a perfect haunt for smugglers who carried their cargo overland from the coast across high Forest tracks, following the old packhorse trails, before unloading and stowing away their goods beneath ancient oaks and beeches; nearby Beggars' Bush, with its clumps of hollies, was a favoured hiding place, Howlers Oak (the illegal exporters of wool were known as owlers) and the Rookery take their names from the smugglers' activities. Harry Walter recalls hearing 'of a man living near Fairwarp who used to ride horseback and sometimes walk down to a receiver from the French boats at Cuckmere Gap and bring back a keg of spirits to be retailed to people who could be trusted not to talk. I have heard my mother say a half pint of brandy could be bought fullproof for a shilling. Two of my forebears were on the Forest where they found several kegs of spirits hidden waiting till someone called for them. They helped themselves to one but did not take it home at the time, but hid it in another safe place – they thought – but they must have been watched for when they went for it later it was missing, and all the rest cleared.' Shepherds were often employed as lookout men for the smugglers, in return for a gift of brandy. They would stand still and silent, apparently watching their sheep, but when a run was being made in the daylight they would hold their crooks in such a way that the smugglers knew whether it was safe or not to proceed. In 1721 several members of the notorious Mayfield gang of smugglers were caught in Cackle Street, and taken to Horsham Gaol where they were tried and executed.

122. Allen Tyler playing the Organ at Christ Church 1912

Allen was the son of Enoch and Ann Tyler and was brought up at Whitehouse Farm. He joined the army and fought in the Boer War; his letter home from Pretoria, dated 6 June 1900, gives a vivid account of the conflict in South Africa: 'It was about 9 o'clock when the Boers started firing on us, but we soon shifted them and drove them out. We drove them from two positions before we got to their forts, and firing commenced in earnest. Captain Brassey had his horse shot from under him, and one of our chaps had a bullet through the fleshy part of his leg, but otherwise the 69th (thought to be the Sussex Yeomanry) came out well, and the Captain has since expressed his satisfaction at our behaviour under fire . . . We camped next to the Sussex Regiment on the night of the fight. I saw two men from East Grinstead whom I know, so of course we had a good chat. The weather here is lovely, not too hot, but it is very cold at night. I sleep with my head in my balaclava helmet and my field service cap over it, so I managed to keep nice and warm. We are told that we shall most likely be disbanded as soon as peace is proclaimed. Every soldier has had enough of it, and wants to be home again . . . Our Captain wanted the names of all those who wish to stay out here when the war is over. There were a lot gave their names in but not I; England is the place for me when it is over.' Allen returned home after the war and settled in Fairwarp with his wife and children and became the organist at Christchurch.

123. Albert Ridley of Old Forge Farm 1912

Albert was the brother of Bicycle Ridley of Nutley and shared with him a passion for all things mechanical. Albert's genius was for invention and he spent many years developing a flying machine based on a bicycle which crashed on its maiden flight into a hedge at the bottom of Fairwarp hill.

124. Lampool 1914

Also known as The Pool or The Hole House and probably derived from 'loam pool', the Subsidy Roll of 1332 records Simon at Hole as landowner at Lampool, making this one of the oldest inhabited sites in the parish. In 1570, it was the property of John Kydder, or Kidder, a distinguished family who lived at Lampool until 1724; later it was owned by the Hothes and then the Newnhams when it became part of Maresfield Park. Rough caves hewn out of the solid sandstone outcrops found in the area were used by smugglers to conceal their bounty; in 1889 three farm labourers from Fairwarp went missing for days and were eventually found lying in a cave near Flittertbanks Farm, unconcious from the effects of the fine French brandy they had uncovered there.

125. The Old Workhouse 1910

The long, two-and-a-half storey building once housed the women and children sections of the Maresfield workhouse in its seventeen rooms. It lies just within the bounds of the Forest, south of Fairwarp and fronting onto the Lampool/Hartfield road; the old Roman road runs through the fields behind the house. Unlike other workhouses of the area, this will not have been an Elizabethan establishment, since no land or building permission would have been available within the Forest for any purpose beyond retaining the deer forest until the end of the seventeenth century. The grant was unlikely to have been made until after the court case of 1693 when Forest property was allocated between new purchasers and the old Commoner-tenants. The workhouse closed in the middle of the nineteenth century and became a farmhouse; the names of the workhouse children are still visible on the attic walls.

Mr G. E. Taylor, seen here, rented the house from his uncles, the Messrs Page, who left it to him in 1910.

Crowborough

Crowborough Beacon stands at the eastern edge of Ashdown Forest, the highest point of the Weald at 792 feet; the town that bears its name sprawled untidily at its feet. There are many possible explanations for the etymology of the name; an early version of the name which appeared in 1292 as Cranbergh probably means 'large hill', later spellings are all variants of Crowbarrow, thought to mean 'hill of crows', for there was not much else here until the seventeenth century when crown land on the forest edge was sold for smallholdings in the reign of Charles I. In his 1870 History of Sussex, M.A. Lower declares: 'probably no spot within the country was, a century or two ago, in so uncivilized a condition as this was, with a barren soil, but with grand and picturesque scenery . . . the views can scarcely be equalled in Sussex. Crowborough Warren was formerly a favourite resort for smugglers from the coast, and for wild and legendary interest it cannot be excelled in this part of England.' Change began in the mid-eighteenth century when Sir Henry Fermor, an ironmaster who lived at Walsh Manor in Jarvis Brook, endowed a charity to build a chapel, All Saints, and school on Chapel Hill, completed in 1744, ten years after his death.

One hundred years later, the area consisted of small fields and woodlands, interspersed with small hamlets; the road from Uckfield to Tunbridge Wells was described as 'very bad, being wholly deep loose sand, but the traveller is compensated by the view from Crowborough Beacon Turnpike', which was still bare of trees or houses, although there was a grocer's shop, described as 'miserable', at Crowborough Cross. In 1839 Earl De La Warr, Lord of the Manor on the Forest, built a church of St. John, belonging to the parish of Withyham, which became known as Crowborough Town, and the speculative era seems to have started around 1856 when the Goldsmiths' Company bought up some country estates which they parcelled out as building sites for large Victorian houses. The opening of the railway at Jarvis Brook in 1868 encouraged local growers and farmers to expand their businesses to meet the challenges of the new markets in London. The town began to grow around three small places: Jarvis Brook to the east in a valley near the station, Crowborough Cross, and Crowborough Town to the west on the Forest edge. In 1890, a local doctor, Dr Leeson Prince, wrote a book extolling the beauty and health benefits of the area, and the town was inundated by invalids and others keen to visit 'Scotland in Sussex'. Hotels and houses were built and service industries developed rapidly; many guests stayed on and settled in the area. Around the turn of the century, many of the small farms which had originated with the Crown land sales in Stuart times came on the market, and there was another rush to build expensive houses for the new, wealthy commuter settlement. In 1904 it became a Parish, separated from its ancient neighbour Rotherfield which had, up until that date, been responsible for all its affairs, and in 1907, the town received further endorsement when Sir Arthur Conan Doyle built himself a manor house, Windlesham, on Hurtis Hill, where he wrote many of his famous books and lived until his death in 1930. Before the First World War, the army established a military camp in the area; by the outbreak of the Second World War, the population of this unstructured town was still only 2,000. After 1950, development was rapid and today the town, in spite of its superb site, has lost contact with the Forest.

126. Mr Hudson, Ashdown Forest Reeve 1910

Mr Hudson, manor reeve to Earl De La Warr, is pictured here with a local constable by the entrance to Fielden Road. The new Crowborough golf club can be seen in the background, the modern building replacing an elaborate towered mansion which was demolished in 1907. The road surface looks reasonable by the standards of the day, but it would have been very dusty in the summer and muddy in winter. The Crowborough Beacon turnpike was situated on a piece of waste ground just above the golf club.

127. Five Hundred Acre Wood 1910

The Royal Commission of 1693 decreed an enclosure adjoining Buckhurst Park which became known as Five Hundred Acre Wood, immortalised as the Hundred Aker Wood in A.A. Milne's *Winnie the Pooh*. Here the planting of beautiful groves of beech and oak produced magnificent trees which still lend beauty and grandeur to the local scene between Friar's Gate and Chuck Hatch. A yew tree that stood outside the Five Hundred was known as a spot where smugglers used to hide; a road near St. John's is still called Smugglers Lane.

128. West Kents at Crowborough Warren 1911

The 4th and 5th Kent Regiments, orginally volunteers, became part of the territorial army in 1908, and trained at the army camp established at Crowborough before the First World War. After the outbreak of war, there was a high density of soldiers in the South East and existing army camps were rapidly extended. By October 1914 the camps at Crowborough and Maresfield had 10,000 men. Disease and accidents became real hazzards as the camps grew larger; one soldier at Crowborough was crushed under the wheels of an ammunition wagon, another was drowned in the Mill Pond deep in the Warren. The scenes of battle were barely 160 miles away across the Channel, and the rumble of artillery became in the words of one man 'monotonous and depressing', the British bombardment at the Somme like the constant rumble of thunder.

129. Army Huts from the Warren 1911

130 & 131. New Warren Mill and the Mill Pond c1890

Crowborough Warren was created after the Royal Commission of 1693 decreed that parts of the 13,991 acres of medieval hunting forest should be enclosed for private use, the remaining 6,400 acres to be left in perpetuity for the use and enjoyment of the Commoners. Crowborough Warren, on the eastern fringes of the Forest, was one of the largest awards at 1,425 acres, the area taking its name from the late medieval practice of the breeding of rabbits for meat and skins in warrens or pillow mounds – long banks of earth enclosed by ditches and a perimeter bank. The land was used for arable farming without much success until the early nineteenth century when Edward Frisby Howis, who worked in the City of London, bought the estate. He planted the land with conifers and deciduous trees, enlarged the existing lake by diverting several small watercourses to feed the mill pond, and built an elaborate 50 foot high, five-storey water mill on the site of a former iron furnace. Known as New Mill, it was one of the most modern in the country with a steam engine that enabled the mill to continue working even when the water was low, and it became famous in 1840 as the place where the flour for Queen Victoria's wedding cake was ground, using wheat grown at nearby Redgate Mill. Later it became a sawmill before it fell into disrepair. The huge 20 foot high mill wheel was taken for scrap for use in the Second World War and the building was declared dangerous and demolished, the 5,000 tons of stone used in its construction dispersed to build new urban houses and stone fireplaces. The mill pond, a great sheet of water which had been used for swimming and boating over the century, despite several drownings in the deep cold waters, was breached by a storm in the 1950s and was eventually emptied.

132. Pratt's Mill 1885

Pratt's Mill was one of two windmills in Crowborough; driven by wind and later by steam, it stood on Crowborough Hill and dominated the skyline. It was built in 1861 by Richard Pratt, a Baptist Minister and writer, who brought it from Tunbridge Wells by horse-drawn timbertug. Three years later his eldest son, Jesse, was killed when his frockcoat got caught in the shaft that worked the flour machine. His younger son, Samuel, took over the running of the mill until his death in 1898; some years later, what remained of the building was incorporated into a private house. The fields below the mill were known as Pratt's Bottom.

133. Samuel Pratt 1900

134. St. John's Church 1906

The Church of St. John the Evangelist was built in 1839 by Earl De La Warr as a chapel of ease for St Michael's Church in Withyham. Almost an exact copy of the church built by John Henry Newman at Littlemore, near Oxford, it was known as Crowborough Chapel and the services were performed by a resident curate until St. John's was formed into a district parish in 1871 and the Rev. Edward Otway Herbert was appointed the first vicar. The school opened the following year, and in 1850 Elizabeth, Countess De La Warr, built the almshouses close by the church as a memorial to her eldest son, George John Frederick, Viscount Cantelupe, who died that year. She endowed them with £270 for keeping the fabric in repair: 'There are six dwellings for the reception of six poor persons of the Parish of Withyham, of whom two shall be men and four women . . . the said six poor persons shall be unmarried or widowers or widows of honest report, members of the Church of England and of the age of fifty and upwards . . .' The inmates received £12 each per annum, together with a house and garden.

135. The Common, St. John's 1906

This area of St. John's Common became an army camp during the Second World War; in 1963 it was sold for private woodland and part of it became the Horder Centre.

136. Woodcarting at Friar's Gate 1910

At the Friar's Gate end of Warren Road, a carter loads his horse-drawn wagon with a load of cordwood which would be sawn up for logs.

137. Crowborough Cross 1890

Looking north up the High Street towards the crossroads when it was still called Willetts Cross.

138. The Beacon Hotel 1910

The Beacon was a grand hotel standing in extensive grounds which was demolished to make room for the new houses in Mill Lane and Beacon Road.

139. Beacon Road looking East 1912

140. The Golf Links 1910

The Golf Links, Crowborough.

141. The Mud Hut c1906

The mud hut was thought to have been built on the edge of the golf course with the South Downs in the distance.

142. Crowborough Beacon from King's Standing 1900

King's Standing is a well-known landmark on the Forest, occupying a commanding position at about 685 feet on the high and open ridge which runs northward from Duddleswell. After 1816 it was planted with firs to mark it as one of the five reservations for the rearing of blackcock and pheasant, but unlike the other four - at Gill's Lap, Five Hundred Acres, Crow's Nest and Hollies Down - it was square in shape with a bank and ditch, all the rest being circular enclosures embanked for the purpose. The square plot is marked on the early 1813 Ordnance Survey Map as King James's Standing, and shown in the same form but named Kinges Stand on the special plan prepared for the division and enclosure of the Forest in 1693. An archeological excavation carried out in the late 1920s revealed the remains of a medieval hunting shelter; examination of iron slag found on the site revealed traces of early iron age occupation as an agricultural settlement, an occupation which continued in Roman times, perhaps in connection with the Roman road which passes only 100 yards to the left. Later the site was enlarged, a shelter erected and the lookout hide arranged for the use of hunters in the medieval deer forest, the name suggesting that this was the place where the monarch stood to watch his herds of deer which were driven towards him either to be counted or shot by long or crossbow, a practice which continued at least to King James's time.

The Master Forester was responsible for the maintenance of the Forest lodges, repairs to the pale and the driving of the game. One ruthless and ambitious courtier who held this position in the reign of Henry VIII was Sir Thomas Boleyn, the father of two daughters, Mary and Anne, who in their turn became one the mistress and the other the wife of the King, and it is sometimes claimed that they met for the first time at King's Standing. Later the hunting lodge fell into disrepair and its ruins levelled, the banks remade and the clump of trees planted in the nineteenth century.

143. Gypsies Hop Picking 1910

'There was a woman down Jarvis Brook who had several acres and she used to let the gypsies stay on there. She was married to old Joby Smith, him what they called King of the Gypsies, so I expect it was his land. They had some old railway wagons along the road and the gypsies used to live in them; they was just like little bungalows really, with gardens, the lot. Then you'd get the wagons stopping up there as well - the old bow tops, and sometimes what they called Readings, the real old-fashioned caravans with lots of fancy carvings and all painted up . . . they used to be there right up to hop-picking time, and after the hops, they'd work on local farms doing all the rough work: pulling potatoes, mangels, sugar beet, swedes. They'd work in any weather - frost, rain - bent over double all day' (Gilbert Sargent). Joby Smith was a shrewd and successful gypsy horse-dealer who progressed from wagon-dweller to Crowborough landowner and died in 1955 aged eighty, a respected member of the local business community.

144. Sweet Hawes Church 1900

Given by the Misses Spedding of the Grange in Sweethaws, the church stood at the gates of the house and was served by the clergy of All Saints.

145. Rotherfield from Lime Kiln Farm 1906

Forest Row

During the fourteenth century a new form of woodland village, or waste edge settlement, began to develop around the edge of the Forest. Forest Row, originally a hamlet in the parish of East Grinstead and first mentioned by this name in 1338, grew from a single street of houses bordering the old London to Lewes road. It is possible that these dwellings provided accommodation for the foresters, falconers and gamekeepers employed by the owners of the newly built hunting lodges to care for the game and to preserve the Forest from encroachment; Pilstye, Chequers, Burnt House Cottages, Rose Cottages, Tablehurst are among the sites which can be dated very close to those times. These sites probably changed very little over the next three centuries until after the Restoration, when squatters took their land from the Forest and the turnpike roads were opening up the countryside to travellers, construction being paid for by consortiums of local gentry who sought easy access to London from their recently established country houses. The phenomenon of landed estates burgeoned in the eighteenth century, and almost everywhere metalled roads spread out from London to serve them. A Surrey-Sussex Turnpike Trust was established in 1717, and a road was laid between Southwark in London and Highgate in Forest Row, with a toll house at Highgate Green. The Wych Cross-Offham Turnpike was completed in 1752 and direct access to Lewes and the coast was achieved. The subsequent demands for inns, carriers, smiths, wheelwrights, saddlers, as well as carpenters, masons and gardeners, increased the size of the village and many new houses were built. The imparking of common land, which had started in Elizabethan times, continued apace over the next two centuries and estates like Kidbrooke, Hammerwood and Ashdown Park were transformed into gentlemen's parks. In 1826 it was constituted an ecclesiastical district, and by 1861 it had a population of 1,411. The opening of the East Grinstead to Groombridge railway line in 1866 and the direct road link to London via Oxted which was established in 1882, transformed the village; Forest Row could send its wood, poultry and dairy produce to London. In 1889 the Royal Ashdown Golf Course was opened and the village became a rural retreat for the wealthy who bought up the grand houses and settled there. After the Second World War it became a commuter village for London and the emerging Gatwick airport and the big houses were developed as schools, residential homes and hotels.

146. The Village 1890

The Chequers Inn, a fine fifteenth century, timber framed posting inn built around 1452, is sited behind the paling fence; the part medieval Rose Cottages are in the middle distance. The Inn was thought to be a haunt for the smugglers who made their way from the coast across the Forest by way of many old tracks which the late Ivan Margary re-discovered when he photographed the Forest from the air in the 1930s. For more than three centuries, from the sixteenth to the early nineteenth century, Sussex men and women were deeply involved in smuggling, in many cases as a means of a livelihood or at least to supplement a meagre wage, and the Forest was used to store the contraband until it could be dispersed to London. The old tracks converged on the established gates or hatches as at Legsheath, Tylehurst, Kidbrooke, Highgate and Plawhatch. The Reverend C.N. Sutton, in his 'Historical Notes of Withyham, Hartfield and Ashdown Forest', recalls a tale told to him by an old woman living in a house on the Forest, which was formerly an inn and a meeting-place for smugglers: 'I remember one evening seeing my uncle going full gallop on his grey horse, with the kegs slung over his back, as hard as he could go along the road here, with the Excise Officers riding after him. When he got to the gate going off the Forest he didn't stop to open it, but blest if he didn't go right over it; he did, upon my word! It's as true as I'm sitting here, right over it, kegs and all. When the Excise folk got to the gate they stopped to open it and they never saw no more of uncle. He got right away into the woods.'

The Chequers Inn was also associated with a famous mail coach robbery which took place at Wall Hill in 1801. The mail coach from Brighton to London stopped at the Inn before being waylaid by two robbers who hid some of their bounty in a field near Hartfield. Finally arrested in Liverpool, the two men were tried in London and hung on a gallows erected on the spot where the robbery took place. It was one of the last public hangings to take place in England and was witnessed by three thousand people, among them two very young brothers John and George Gilham (who lived at Spring Cottage in what is now Gilham Lane) whose heads were rubbed on the soles of the feet of the condemned men.

The Village. Forest Row. (2)

Sayer's Bro[s?]
Photo Series

147. The Village Hall 1890

Before the Village Hall was built, a smithy and a single-storey building stood on the site, for many years the forge of the Finch family and possibly established there on manorial waste ground when the 1717 turnpike opened. In 1892, Henry Freshfield, solicitor for the Bank of England and owner of Kidbrooke Park, bought the land and commissioned Job Luxford to build the Hall, effectively dividing the village square into an upper and lower section. To the west of the Hall lies Holy Trinity Church; built of local stone in 1836 on the site of old gravel pits, its distinctive spires covered in slips of wood, originally of oak and now chestnut, called shingles.

148. Queen Victoria's Diamond Jubilee Fountain 1900

To celebrate Queen Victoria's Diamond Jubilee, a fountain was erected at the northern end of the village square; it was removed in the 1950s. The children in the photograph are the offspring of the Reverend George Carnack Fisher, vicar of Forest Row, later Bishop of Southampton and then of Ipswich, who married Mary Penelope Gwendoline Thompson, the only surviving child of Thomas Charles Thompson, owner of Ashdown Park at Wych Cross.

149. The Swan 1876

The oldest part of the Swan Inn dates back to medieval times, with later eighteenth and nineteenth century additions. It traded as an ale-house, providing refreshment for the drovers, traders, pack-horse men, wagoners and smugglers passing through Forest Row, as well as supplying ale for local consumption, becoming the focal point for village entertainment with dancing, music and games. Originally called the Yew Tree after the fine tree which grew behind the timber framed building, it changed its name in the latter half of the eighteenth century, by which time it was a busy inn on the turnpiked roads between London and Brighton, and the spas at Tunbridge Wells. During the mid nineteenth century, Acts of Parliament were passed in an attempt to restrict the hours of opening of public houses, to try to control the growing alchoholism, described so graphically in the novels of Charles Dickens, but the authorities were up against vested interests and entrenched brewers so there were very few hours of the day or night when the pubs were closed. In an attempt to stem the decline, the Church of England Temperance Society and the Band of Hope were founded in Forest Row and attracted as many as 200 members before the First World War, although many of them were children.

150. The Old Forge 1878

The old forge was sited just below The Chequers Inn, on the opposite side of the road to the Swan Inn.

151. Histed Butcher's Shop 1890

The elaborate display was hung outside the shop each day, the dog guarded the meat from other four-legged intruders.

152. Histed Butchers 1906

153. Forest Row Girls' School c1900

Towards the end of the eighteenth century a school was opened by Mr and Mrs James Holman of Yew Tree Cottage, Quaybrook, to educate the poor children of the Forest. Little is known about the school except that naughty boys were suspended by the waist from hooks in the ceiling beams. The first serious attempt to open a school in the village arose when the Rt Hon Charles Abbott, MP, Speaker of the House of Commons, bought the Kidbrooke estate and opened a school which, in 1814, became the Forest Row National School. In 1851, the Lord of the Manor gave a piece of manorial waste ground which became the permanent site for two schools, one for the boys, the other for girls, and Charles Abbott, now Lord Colchester, was able to close his school with its seventy-two pupils in the knowledge that it would be incorporated into the new schools the following year. The teaching programme for the girls was reading, writing, arithmetic, grammar and needlework and, shared with the boys, geography and scripture. The schools were rigorously separated by segregated entrances at each end of the building, one sex classrooms and playgrounds. In 1878 Thomas and Betsy Bishop were appointed heads; Mrs Bishop's entries in the school Log Book were full of concern for the lamentable state of the girls' education and displayed a lack of understanding for the poverty and deprivation suffered by her pupils: 'First standard children are of an unusually dull intellect owing to the manner in which they are brought up. Their homes are scattered widely about the Forest or at some remote spot in the fields . . . we feel our task is hopeless.' She notes children coming to school for the first time at any age between seven and fourteen years without any knowledge of the three Rs and some knowing nothing of the alphabet. Absenteeism for hay, corn, hop and fruit harvests were a regular procedure, the girls had to stay at home to mind the new baby or help mother: 'No compulsion is in reality exercised here . . . and as no fixed fines are inflicted the parents laugh at the Education Act . . .' The years towards the end of the century were affected by particularly severe, wintry weather which prevented children attending a school singularly lacking in heating; epidemics of diptheria, measles, scarlet fever and even smallpox added to the absences and, occasionally, the death toll.

Top row: fourth from left, Nelly Parker

Second row: second from right, Frances Bishop

Third row: second from left, Hetty Weeding; *fourth from left,* Edith Parker; *sixth from left,* Edith Bishop

Front row: extreme right, Ernest Bishop. The only boy in the Girls' School, Ernest looks very young, and records shown that he was born in 1898. His father, Samuel, was a builder and plumber who started the hardware store which bore his name and, perhaps mindful of the benefits an early education would give his son, enrolled him as soon as he could. Ernest later developed his father's hardware enterprise into a thriving business.

154. Brambletye Castle 1886

Brambletye is one of only two sites in Forest Row mentioned in the Domesday Book; there are no remains of that occupation, but instead the ruins of a Jacobean mansion whose last occupants fled the country 250 years ago under suspicion of treason. It is also the site of an earlier Tudor moated manor house and farmhouse, a fifteenth century forge and a seventeenth century barn.

155. Kidbrooke Park 1901

An extensive survey of the Forest in 1564 names Kidbrooke Gate by Forest Row near the bottom of Priory Road where the Medway runs small and narrow; the name has three possible derivations, the first kite brook after the bird that was common to the Forest, the second to the Kidder family of Maresfield who were bailiffs to Lancaster Great Park for many generations, and the third that the area was used by the game reeves for rearing young deer. The land was bought in 1734 by William Nevill, who had become the 42nd Lord Abergavenny on the death of a cousin, and he built a mansion of local iron-stained sandstone; the following year he enlarged the estate by obtaining a further 108 acres from the Duke of Dorset. By 1790 the family seat at Eridge had been restored and the Abergavennys moved back; in 1803 Kidbrooke was bought by the Rt Hon Charles Abbott, MP, Speaker of the House of Commons and later Lord Colchester. He employed Humphrey Repton to re-design the park, and made good use of available natural resources. George Tester, who worked at Kidbrooke, described to William Augustus Raper how Abbott had 'made an artificial cascade in the brook (presumably the Medway) and took all the largest stones he could find on the neighbouring Forest for this purpose. I helped with one stone weighed nine tons, and we dragged it down in a truck made on purpose at Forest Row and drawn by seven pair of oxen. We also took many loads of green turf off the Forest to make his lawns and gravel to make his carriage roads.' The Abbotts continued to live at Kidbrooke until 1874, when it was bought by Henry Freshfield, who later became the first Chairman of the Board of Conservators of Ashdown Forest; his son, Douglas, built Wych Cross Place. It was sold to the Kekewich family who were at Kidbrooke for a very short time (1909-1915) but they left behind strong associations with the Boy Scouts, the Cadet Corps and the Queen's Nurses, as well as tragedy, for the War Memorials bear the names of three of their four sons. During the last years of the war, Kidbrooke became a base camp; in 1921 it was bought by the Norwegian banker, Olaf Hambro and was the setting in 1929 for the 'Pageant of Ashdown Forest', a glorious production with verses especially written by Vita Sackville-West and A.A. Milne, and a cast starring a number of luminaries of the day, including a nine-year-old Christopher Milne. It was the swansong for Kidbrooke Park; by 1938 it was no longer in private ownership, and later became the Michael Hall Rudolf Steiner School.

BURNT HOUSE COTTAGES FORST ROW

156. Burnt House Cottages 1900

Originally the site for three cottages, the remaining two are typical examples of the rebuilding in the weald during the period 1570-1630, when increased prosperity enabled people to build timber framed houses of this kind and do away with the hovels which had formerly served as shelters for labourers.

157. Chapel Lane 1908

Chapel Lane was a small, interconecting road, no more than a dirt track, dusty in the dry weather and a rutted quagmire after prolonged rain. Formerly Plawes Lane, it was originally named after Plawes Gate at its entrance to the Forest and has been in use for hundreds of years; since it was metalled by the County Council in 1901 it has been known as Chapel Lane. During the nineteenth century it was used for the extraction of timber, stone, gravel, turf and bedding from the Forest for use on the estates, farms and small-holdings of the Medway valley. In the latter part of the nineteenth century, a sawpit was in use just above Little Shalesbrook Cottage, where about fifteen men were engaged in timber work, coopering and lath-making. In 1826 the then Lord Abergavenny remarked on the continuous woodland he could see as he stood at the top of Chapel Lane looking towards Coleman's Hatch. The timber trades: hoop and broom making, charcoal burning, and the need for timber for the trenches in the First World War, radically changed this vision of Lord Abergavenny.

158. Hartfield Road from Chapel Lane 1895

Hartfield Road became of major importance when the Earl of Dorset made his home at Buckhurst, Withyham in the early Stuart times. The turnpike road opened in 1788, with a toll house on the site of Sheridan House on the Green. The turnpike controllers were expected to collect tolls from all road users: carriages, horsemen, wagons, cattle and sheep drovers, and these charges were greatly resented by many of the farmers and poorer people who could ill afford the tax. Many people took evasive action and used other routes, or created their own tracks, to avoid the toll gates. The Turnpike Trusts enjoyed a bonanza until the railway era began for the South

East in 1841, and by the late 1880s the County Councils had taken over their roads and bridges, dismantling the toll gates and demolishing some of the toll houses, although the one at Highgate is a private house.

The builder's yard in the foreground belonged to James Waters, son of James and Mary and brother to Isaac, who founded his eponymous building firm which ran successfully in tandem with that of his younger brother's, and later with his nephews, Harry and Edgar (H. & E.) Waters.

159. Three Generations 1905

Three generations of one family pose for this portrait. On the right, a one-armed Mr Longley stands next to Mr Saunders, his grandson, Jack, in front of him. As a grown man, Jack ran the newsagent shop in the village.

160 & 161. The Royal Ashdown Golf Club 1908

The club was only the second to open in the county of Sussex and was formed after a meeting of founder members at the Brambletye Castle Hotel in December 1888, attended by a large number of local people who were persuaded by the Secretary, R.W.P. Birch, that Forest Row would benefit from the increasing trade and that the club would provide a means of employment for men and boys. He also reported that the London, Brighton and South Coast Railway had agreed to run special and convenient trains for the golf parties, but what he did not say, or perhaps anticipate but which nevertheless happened, was the increase in building and population which took place because of the Golf Course opening, and the establishment of the direct rail route to London in 1882. The population of the village grew from 1,817 in 1878 to 2,561 in 1905, a forty per cent increase in twenty-seven years. The original club house, at Bank Farm, was rented and the *Sussex Daily News* described it as 'a picturesque farmhouse with lath and plaster walls and oaken beams'. An event in the summer of 1893 led to the Club aquiring the Royal appellation when the Duke of Cambridge reviewed his troops encamped on the Forest. He was asked to drive a ball off the green which he did, dressed in full uniform, thus giving the Club its royal charter. The present Club House was built by Isaac Waters, founder of the Forest Row

building and contracting firm, and opened in 1894; two years later he built the Ladies Golf Club House for £742. In 'The Golf Courses of the British Isles', published in 1910, Bernard Darwin writes: 'The Ashdown Forest course lies in that most delightful but alas! most rapidly built-over country near Forest Row and East Grinstead, and not very far from Crowborough where is another very charming course. Like Eastbourne, it can boast of some very curly and puzzling putting greens, but there the resemblance ends. It lies not upon the downs, but upon the forest, which means among the heather, and alone of all the heathery clan, indeed almost alone among golf courses, it is as nearly as may be perfectly natural. Nature, a really wonderfully good architect, has been kind in supplying a variety of pits and streams to carry . . . there flows at the bottom of the valley a stream that shall engulf the feebly struck ball, to say nothing of heather and bracken and other things'.

162. The Founding Members c1891

A very early group photograph of the founding members of the Golf Club, showing a corner of the original club house. Seated in the centre, from left to right: H. Lucas, R.W.P Birch, T. Hyde, H. Jeddere-Fisher, Rev. C.C. Woodland and Dr Magrath, the treasurer.

163. Army Camp 1893

This camp is believed to have been the one inspected and reviewed by the Duke of Cambridge in the summer of 1893. Kidbrooke Park is just visible in the trees beyond the dusty track which is now the main road into Forest Row.

164. Broadstone Farm 1909

Will no one deign a walk, to treat the eye,
To Broadstone bower from classic Brambletye;
To beauteous scenes that on the vision swell,
The heath-crown'd mountain and the lonely dell.
In these retreats how much the bosom warms
With lovely Nature in her wildest charms.
Or let the tourist seek the foot-bridge vale
Where gentle osiers bend before the gale,
An open space before the stream is found,
Where the bold forest stands in grandeur round;
A sylvan amphitheatre is seen
In light and shade with varied tints between;
The beech, the oak and all the forest store,
If these don't please him I will chose no more.
This was the spot, and far from beaten road,
My honour'd parents chose for their abode;
Here to pursue through each succeeding day,
Their rural cares in life's uncertain way.

Part of an epic poem written in 1865 by John Turley on the occasion of his visit to Broadstone House, the place of his birth, and supposed to have been spoken on the spot.

The estate known today as Broadstone Farm started life as Broadstone Walk, one of the medieval walks of the old deer Park. Following the division of the Forest by the Duchy of Lancaster Decree of 1693, Broadstone was held by Alexander Staples, one of the Forest developers, who attempted to develop it as an area of rabbit production. In 1906 it was bought by Walter Johnson, a businessman whose engineering firm Johnson & Phillips brought him great prosperity, and he built a large Victorian-type house, which was demolished in 1953 due to army damage, and set up two narrow-gauge electric railways on the estate which was now about 150 acres in extent. The present farmhouse is thought to date back to the early sixteenth century when Sir Thomas Boleyn incurred costs of £27 for making five new Forest lodges, and could be on the site of an earlier, medieval building.

Benjamin Potter, a jack of all trades who lived for many years at Quaybrook and later wrote his life story in a large account book of about 500 pages which gives a fascinating record of a labourer's life in turn-of-the-century Sussex, started working at Broadstone Farm in 1900 when he was a boy of fourteen: 'I got a job as a carter boy with a team of three horses at Broadstone Farm, at four shillings per week, this place was also a large pheasant rearing farm, employing one head and one under gamekeeper, it was situated right on the edge of Broadstone Warren on two sides and Ashdown Forest on the other two, there were just two houses together and various buildings, not another house within half a mile of it . . . The carter soon learnt me how to do two things, one was to drive three horses perfectly at plough, the other how to smoke both a pipe and cigarettes, and although I think it made me look manly with a pipe stuck in my gills, I daresay truthfully I looked more a fool . . . I think I was much more thrilled with the Keeper's side than the farming, as there were pheasants almost everywhere, they reared them by the thousand, there was a great barn full of rows and rows of nest boxes all round the inside stacked one above the other . . .'

165. Quaybrook 1898

Job Luxford, builder of the Village Hall, had his brickyard at Shepherd's Hill, Quaybrook, producing both kiln and clamp-fired bricks, tiles and drainpipes before H. & E. Waters took it over in 1918 and incorporated it into their business.

166. The Broomyard, Highgate Green 1912

From 1723 onwards, the toll-house at Highgate controlled the turnpike road where a number of tracks converged, often no more than dirt tracks wide enough for a single cart. Before development of the area started in 1873, there were fewer than six established buildings which included Chequer Farm, the Royal Oak beerhouse, Forest House and the Broomyard. Birch was the chief material for the brooms, although heather was also used but not so frequently because it lasted too well; the birch twigs were cut in the winter before the rising of the sap in local woods where carting was done with a horse and wagon. When the loaded wagon arrived at the yard, birch stacks were built against the boundary of Royal Oak Cottages, criss-crossed and roofed to resist the weather, sometimes to a height of 30 foot. Throughout the year men were making brooms in the sheds, one employed making handles from chestnut and hazel or, if in short supply, ash and hornbeam, another assembling the birch boughs trimmed to a uniform length and bonded with cane, hazel or wire. One man could make six or eight dozen wire-bonded brooms, or four dozen cane-bonded brooms in a day. The trimmings of the birch were made into charcoal and taken to Latham's in London where they were sold to hospitals for keeping warm food trolleys; peaboughs, beanpoles and firewood produced by the yard were sold locally. The Broomyard flourished under the control of Abraham Card who took it over after his father's death in 1894, and during his time it earned the appellation By Appointment to His Majesty's Government; at its most productive the yard was producing 200 dozen brooms per week. As the demand for brooms declined, the yard reduced its workforce accordingly until it was closed finally in September 1977.

167. The Weir on the Medway 1910

The weir was constructed for the mill pond at Tablehurst.

168. Tablehurst Mill 1900

The corn mill at Tablehurst was built on a late medieval site; an ancient ridgeway may have crossed the Medway at this point by the old track discovered by Ivan Margery in 1929.

169. Trimmer's Pond 1880

Trimmer's Pond is a wealden hall house dating back to the thirteenth century which stood on the banks of the Medway. It was in a ruined state when, in the 1920s, it was bought by Mr. F.J. Nettlefold, the new owner of Chelwood Vachery. With the help of the Sussex Archeological Society and the builders H. & E. Waters, it was dismantled and transported to the grounds of the Vachery where it was re-erected with the greatest care and attention.

170. The Hoopyard 1900

The old hoopyard stood in Chapel Meadow and the craft of making wooden hoops for wooden barrels was at its height in the nineteenth century when export to the rest of the world became possible. There were two kinds of barrels: the slack type to carry dry goods such as flour, apples, cheese, cement, etc., and the dry type for carrying liquids such as beer, wine, vinegar. Millions of hoops were needed to keep these barrels tight and the wood favoured for its suppleness was hazel, although chestnut, oak and ash were also used. A good workman could produce six hundred hoops a day and many were sent to the West Indies for use in the sugar and rum trade. The hoopmaker's trade began to decline when cheaper hoops were imported from Western Europe, and finally died out when metal bands replaced the wooden ones after the First World War.

171. Ashdown House 1910

Ashdown House stands on an ancient thirteenth century site, known until 1794 as Lavortie, from an Anglo-Saxon name, lawerceteag, meaning a lark-frequented enclosure. It seems likely that it was a sub-manor of Brambletye which had its own entry in the Domesday survey of 1085 and was gifted by King William to the Count of Mortain, his half-brother, after the Conquest. The Newnham family of Maresfield Park were the last to own the estate before it became known as Ashdown House; they bought it, with five hundred acres of land, in 1690. Just over one hundred years later it became the property of John Trayton Fuller who embarked upon the project of constructing a new and grander house; he enlisted the help of a young and almost untried architect, Benjamin Henry Latrobe, who was soon to make his mark in America. Born in Yorkshire in 1764, Latrobe was given the commission to design Hammerwood, just two miles away, when he was only twenty eight years old, and Ashdown House two years later. In his book, 'Architecture of Southern England', John Julius Norwich describes the house as 'a gem, all Ionic, feminine grace', while Nikolaus Pevsner declares it 'very perfect indeed'. Latrobe emigrated to America in 1795, where he has since been considered the first professional architect in the United States. Often credited with the building of the White House in Washington, that honour belongs to an Irishman named James Hoban, although Latrobe did a great deal of work on the original plans; the Cathedral in Baltimore is considered to be his finest work, and in 1803 he was appointed Surveyor of the Public Buildings of the United States by President Thomas Jefferson.

The Fullers were to live at Ashdown for the next seventy years, increasing the size of the estate. In 1886, two brothers from Brighton, William Randall Lee and Francis Archer Lee, who had helped their father run a school for the sons of gentlemen in Brighton known as Connaught House, leased the house and founded a boys' preparatory school. Both in their early thirties, they shared a passion for golf and were both instrumental in the foundation of the Royal Ashdown Golf Club. In 1910 William Lee handed the school over to his niece and her schoolmaster husband, and the fortunes of the school started to rise along with the pupil numbers which increased from twelve to fifty-seven during their twenty-nine year stewardship. Today it is a successful co-educational boarding school for over 200 pupils.

172. Thomsett's Bank 1910

One of the smallest awards granted by the Royal Commission of 1693 was one- and-a-half acres to Widow Thomsett for her enclosure on a bank by a small stream that runs into the Medway east of Forest Row where her name is still commemorated today.

173. Tom Tit's Lane 1910

Tom Tit's Lane was a dirt track of some antiquity and the name is thought to be an analogy of Thompsett's Lane. Formerly it was Inkpen Lane (named after William Inkpen who lived in the cottage now known as Oakmead), Waters Lane and Pig Lane after H. & E. Waters and their pig farm on its western side.

Coleman's Hatch

Coleman's Hatch, an early recorded settlement on the margins of the Forest, is another example of a fourteenth century waste-edge woodland village, a formless hamlet with cottages dispersed sporadically at the sites of springs. Its church is twentieth century, built in 1913 in the Early English style; prior to that the villagers had worshiped at the parish church in Hartfield or at the church dedicated to St. Richard de Wych built by Thomas Charles Thompson in the grounds of his private estate at Ashdown Park.

Holy Trinity Church, Coleman's Hatch

174. Holy Trinity Church 1914

175 & 176. Newbridge 1908

Newbridge was the first wealden ironworks to produce cast iron by the new process of blasting; in 1496 when Henry VII moved to prevent a Scottish invasion, he granted a commission to one Henry Fyner for the supply of arms which he would make at Newbridge. He was given funds to pay workers, called by then *founders,* and ordered to 'construct a mill and forges with a great hammer and wheel for to make steel...' on six acres of land with a watercourse; blast furnaces needed a good head of water to operate the water wheels which drove the bellows for the furnace and the hammers for the forge, and the streams which rushed down the steep, incised valleys or ghylls of the Forest were collected into ponds during the winter, for use by the forge in a dry summer. French experts were enlisted – cast iron was in production on the Continent at a much earlier date – and a small colony of French ironworkers lived in scattering of tile-clad or weather-boarded cottages, lying around the slopes overlooking the natural hollow where the mill waters were collected from a dozen different sources. The ironworkers became squatters, their cottages developed into permanent hamlets, a pattern that was repeated along the fringes of the Forest. Newbridge clearly became a complex of ironworks for, in 1658 by which time iron working had ceased, old hammers, furnace ponds, bays and other buildings used in the industry still existed. Moss Cottage, seen here, was originally three cottages and was reputed to have been an ale house in the fifteenth and sixteenth centuries.

177. Kidd's Hill 1894

The banks of the dam or bay at Newbridge, a rather curious circular shape, can still be seen to the left of this photograph at the bottom of Kidd's Hill, just before the Newbridge Splash. The new bridge (hence the name) spanned the leat which fed water from the weir to the mill wheel and there are still scatterings of slag in the stream. The hill took its name from a Captain Kidd who owned New Lodge in the mid-nineteenth century.

178. A Cottage at Newbridge 1894

A well-known Forest character, George 'Grevious' Heasman, lived in a shack in the garden of this cottage which belonged to a relative. Proud of the fact that he had never worked in his life, he eked out a living poaching pheasants, hares, rabbits and deer from Forest and private estate alike, making wine from gorse, flowers and vegetables, and selling lost golf balls, retrieved by well trained dogs, to a dealer from Brighton.

179 & 180. Newbridge Mill 1893

Virtually all the water mills around the Forest were originally hammer mills and subsequently became corn mills. The main furnace at Newbridge was later used as a corn mill, and the building shown here was built after the closure of the ironworks. The spillway and one of the hammer ponds, partially reclaimed, still exist, a beautiful legacy of the industry that once dominated the Forest.

181. Gill's Lap 1900

The clump of Scots Pine were planted at Gill's Lap in 1816 for the breeding of game birds. When it matured, the outline viewed from a distance represented a single-hump camel and in the 1930s it was sometimes referred to as the Camel's Hump. Gill's Lap is pronounced by local dwellers as *Jill's*, although the name changes in the Forest records throughout the centuries; sometimes Gill's Cap, Ghylls Clump, Gill's Leap from the Saxon name meaning 'leap of the hind'. In the 1658 survey, the reference is spelled with a J indicating that although spelling was erratic at the time, that was the correct pronounciation. There is evidence of a Celtic enclosure some 900 yards south-east of the clump; pottery found there makes it certain that the place existed in the early Iron Age and was probably constructed at that time, most likely as a cattle enclosure or agricultural settlement. From this point on the Forest, with its high sightings on all sides, it is possible on a clear day to see from the North to the South Downs, a distance of some forty miles, and to see the Thames estuary at Rochester. It is an enchanted place and one that inspired A.A. Milne, when he was living below at Cotchford, who renamed it Galleon's Lap in his famous stories about Winnie the Pooh and his friends.

182. Gill's Lap and Kidd's Hill 1910

183. View from Kidd's Hill 1904

A panoramic view of the Forest from the top of Kidd's Hill looking towards the Coleman's Hatch/Hartfield ridge.

184. Cottages at Coleman's Hatch 1900

Yew Tree Cottage is to the left, Forest View in the middle right, and the golf course can be seen in the distance.

185. Forest Cottage 1910

186. Holly Hill 1895

Holly Hill was the home of Bernard Hale, Deputy-Lieutenant of Sussex, Chairman of the East Grinstead Bench of Magistrates and litigant in the famous test case brought in 1876 by the Earl De La Warr, Lord of the Manor of Duddleswell and owner of the Forest. One of his tenant farmers, John Miles of Possingford Farm, was scything litter in the autumn of that year while his wife was cutting bracken, when the Earl's keeper, William Pilbeam, arrived on the scene and ordered them to stop. His advise was ignored, 'I continued to cut' reported John Miles, and shortly afterwards a letter went out to all Commoners from the Earl's solicitors which stated that their client did not accept the rights of the Commoners to cut litter on the Forest and cart it away, and the practice must therefore cease forthwith. As far back as 1693 the then Lord of the Manor had agreed that Commoners may graze their cattle on the Forest, but there had never been any mention that they may remove anything, although for generations Commoners and non-Commoners alike had taken almost anything they could get into a cart including stone, gravel, marl, sand, peat, turf and litter; the poor earned a living from it, and the rich built fine houses and gardens for no, or little, payment. Holly Hill itself did rather well from the Forest; in 1827 John Booker was working for the estate and was engaged in removing about an acre of turf to make lawns, and many loads of peaty turf for rhododendrons and flower beds. The next owner had large quantities of stone for building stables. Heather was used for thatching, gravel for filling bottoms of yards and garden paths, and for many years the greenhouses were heated by burning peat cut from Newbridge. For many years prior to 1876, great fears had been expressed that there would be nothing left of the Forest if things continued as they were, and it was on this that his Lordship was basing his case; in retrospect, he seems to have been rather long suffering.

Other Commoners who had an interest in the case included Henry Fitzalan Howard, 15th Duke of Norfolk, the third Earl of Sheffield, the third Baron Colchester, Sir Spencer Maryon-Wilson - hardly small farmers or humble labourers - and a number of men who could neither read nor write. Bernard Hale employed William Augustus Raper, a partner in a firm of Battle solicitors, to contest the action. He advised that as litter had been removed by Commoners for very many years, it would be helpful if they could find as many witnesses as possible to testify to this effect, and for the next year or so he visited the old foresters in their homes, gathering information and statements from living witnesses which he collected into great volumes, now known as The Raper Papers; recollections which quite apart from their value at that time, give the sharpest possible impression of a poor man's life on the Forest from the beginning of the nineteenth century. The case was heard eventually in the High Court of Justice and after many weeks of debate, judgement was pronounced in favour of the Lord of the Manor. It was a severe blow to the Commoners, but it it said that Sussex folk will not be 'druv', and at an appeal hearing in 1881, the judgement was reversed. It was agreed that a Board of Conservators should be set up, elected by the Commoners, and charged with the duties of safeguarding the rights of the Commoner, guarding against encroachments and preserving the Forest in its natural condition. In 1885 an Act of Parliament authorised the Board to pass the necessary bye-laws to regulate the Forest.

187. The Hatch Inn 1905

The Hatch Inn was originally a row of three cottages said to date back to 1430, which means they were there before the Newbridge furnaces were blowing and might well in due course have housed their workers. It was not until the eighteenth century that the cottages became an inn, called at that time The Cock; or was *chark* the word used and then corrupted by time, for a landlord tells of its use by charcoal burners, who came toiling up the long hill for refreshment. Later it became The Hatch to commemorate the original coalman's gate onto the Forest in the days of the Newbridge furnace (hence Coleman's Hatch), and it was claimed as a haunt for smugglers with rum its speciality and Captain Kidd its mastermind, although there is little proof of this last fact. Certainly the Inn looks the part, low, rather dark and hugged into the landscape; a mysterious place with secrets to confide. There was a forge by the Inn; in the early nineteenth century the blacksmith was father to Martha Langridge, who later become William Augustus Raper's 'excellent witness' in the famous test case brought by Earl De La Warr against John Miles which eventually led to the formation of a Board of Conservators in 1885. In later life she recalled her early years on the Forest: 'The first year we were at Coleman's Hatch, 1817, my mother and I and the other children cut loads of bracken on the Forest – 3 for Col. Young, 3 for Mr George Atkins of Newbridge Mill and 3 for ourselves; they paid us 10/- a load for cutting. I remember the occasion because we took the baby in its cradle out on the Forest and my sister and I upset it between us. My father was one who bit before he barked and he gave me and my sister a good hiding when we got home. My father used to cut a great deal of peat from the bog near Newbridge. I used to help him lay out the pieces and I remember one occasion when so engaged falling into the water there and getting into a dreadful mess. I was frightened by the efts (newts) swimming over my arm and when I got out father boxed my ears.'

Withyham and Hartfield

The Hundred of Hertevel was mentioned in the Domesday Survey of 1085 as the property of Robert, Earl of Mortain and half brother to King William, who received very large and valuable grants, among which was the extensive Forest of Ashdown and its adjacent manor. The area was about 17,500 acres and it stretched to Rotherfield, Rushmonden, East Grinstead and the border of Kent and consisted mostly of thick wood with the river Medway flowing through them. Only a few acres, enough for twenty-two ploughs, were cleared and cultivated, probably near the river. Pigs found grazing in the forests and eels were plentiful in the river and ponds. The people were poor; most were villeins, ie workers permanently tied to the owners of the land, but some were bordars, that is, cottagers of some independence. Withyham means the enclosures of withies of willows; the name Hartfield implies the existence, in former times, of a preserve for deer and the village is the site of some ancient defence: 'The Barons of Pevensy had their hunting seats at Hartfield and Maresfield. For, though ruins exist in either of these localities, there is a field to the north of the village of Hartfield called the Castle Field, the unevenness of which, and a large mound standing about the centre of it, clearly show that a small castle once stood upon this spot, the foundations of which might possibly, if searched for, still be discovered beneath the surface' (Rev. C.N. Sutton). George Bulleyn of Hartefeild (probably of the Hever Castle family) was listed as iron master in the Return of 1574; a forge at Lower Parrock supplied 9 tons of gunstones (cannon balls) to Henry VIII in 1515 and it is possible that the ones found on the *Mary Rose* when it was raised from the Solent in 1982 were cast in Hartfield or at Newbridge.

188. Old Buckhurst 1900

The valient knights who accompanied the Conqueror into England in 1066 were largely rewarded for their help in placing him upon the throne. Among them was Robert de Dene who became Lord of Buckhurst, which Manor was brought into the Sackville family by the marriage of Sir Jordan de Sackville with Lady Ela de Dene in the twelfth century; the family became prosperous and influential over the following centuries, connected by marriage to royalty when John Sackville MP and Sheriff of the Counties of Sussex and Surrey, married Margaret Boleyn of Hever Castle, sister to Anne, in 1532. Thomas Sackville, born at Buckhurst in 1536, became Lord High Treasurer to Elizabeth I who raised him to the peerage and granted him the magnificent former Archbishop's Palace at Knole in Kent; later he became the first Earl of Dorset under James I. He was also a distiguished Elizabethan poet and playwright who gave England its first classic tragedy, 'Gorboduc'. His ancient home, Old Buckhurst, which was first mentioned in the Enquiry of 1274 but is thought to have Saxon origins, was abandoned in favour of Knole and the house fell into ruin. It is from Old Buckhurst that a member of the Sackville family bore news to Mary, Queen of Scots, of her impending execution. Of the six original towers, only one remains, and this was evidently the principal entrance as the Arms of the Sackville family and the letters A.I. are on the face of it. The ancient stonework was taken to East Grinstead for use in the building of Sackville College in 1616 by Richard, third Earl of Dorset. The old house opposite the tower, now known as Old Buckhurst, dates back to the reign of Henry VII.

After three centuries of ownership by the Crown as a possession of the Duchy of Lancaster, Ashdown was disafforested by letters patent of Charles II after the Restoration and granted, in 1671, first to the Earl of Bristol and then to the Earl of Dorset, whose efforts to enclose and

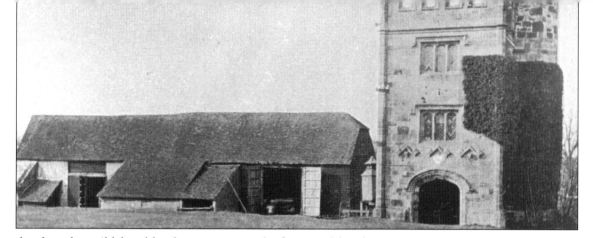

develop the wild heathland were constantly frustrated by the 'crossness of the neighbourhood'. Under the Settlement made in 1693, following a lawsuit involving Charles Sackville, the sixth Earl of Dorset, against John Newnham and other Commoners, 6,400 acres were declared subject to rights of common, and so remain to this day. Sucessive Dukes of Dorset, as Lords of the Manor of Duddleswell, remained owners of the soil until, with the extinction of the male line in 1815, it passed to their successor in title by marriage, Earl De La Warr. The feudal link was broken in 1988 when the tenth Earl De La Warr sold the freehold of Ashdown Forest to East Sussex County Council for just over one million pounds.

189. Buckhurst Park 1910

Buckhurst, the present seat of the eleventh Earl De La Warr, was originally called Stoneland Lodge and was leased to the ironworker, John Baker, who owned Duckings House, in 1509. The oldest part of the present house dates back to 1743 and this was retained when, in 1830, the fifth Earl De La Warr, George John Sackville West, had most of the old house pulled down and employed the architect Repton to build the new house, Buckhurst. By the large lake, which is fed by two streams of the Medway, is an oak tree planted by Queen Victoria in 1835; on the birthdays of the Earl and Countess De La Warr, a salute was always fired across the lake by their private battery of fourteen guns. Only seven of the guns were fired when the children had a birthday, except in the case of the eldest son, Lord Buckhurst, in whose honour the full battery of fourteen cannon would blaze across the water. The De La Warr children amused themselves by using the guns for target practice, but their shooting was not always accurate and after a shot had penetrated Hartfield High Street, the Earl intervened and the battery was silenced forever.

190. Duckings 1911

Duckings is a very fine ironmaster's Wealden house built in the sixteenth century by John Baker of Mayfield who worked the furnace and forge on the nearby Stonelands estate. In 1570 the house passed to the Sackvilles and from 1684 to 1910 it was leased to the Hall family; this is considered to be the longest lease ever held in England.

191. The Dorset Arms 1910

Four hundred years ago the Dorset Arms was Somers Farm House and owned much of the adjoining land; the first recorded date of it being used as an ale house comes in 1636 when William Pigott of Witham was listed as a Sussex tavern-keeper.

192. Withyham Church and Rectory 1912

There have been rectors at Withyham since 1328, and the church has suffered over the centuries variously at the hands of Kings Henry VIII and Edward VI, the restrictions of Puritan fanaticism and most devastatingly by a fire in 1663 which 'burnt (it) down by a tempest of thundering and lightning'. The church restoration appears, from the date on the old sun dial over the south porch, to have been completed in 1672. One of the interesting features is the Sackville chapel, built by Richard, third Earl of Dorset in 1624, which is a shrine to the ruling family and contains monuments by some of the finest sculptors of the day. The Rectory is beautifully sited on a knoll close to the church, seventy-two feet above the lake, with extensive views over the Forest. The house can be traced back in the Barony of Buckhurst more than four hundred years and there is a 1785 drawing of it in the British Museum. The verandah was added after 1800 by the Rev. Sackville Stephens Bale; the oak panelling in the drawing room dates back to Henry VII and came from Brambletye Castle.

hyham Church & Rectory.

urch & Schools, Hartfield.

193. Hartfield Church and School 1898

The parish church of St. Mary the Virgin dates back to the thirteenth century, but as Hartfield is mentioned in the Domesday Survey there will probably have been a church there at that time, possibly made of wood. The north wall is the oldest part of the church; in the fourteenth century a tower was added and also a chantry chapel on the south side. The tower, with its shingled spire, is thought to be fifteenth century; large scale restoration work was undertaken in the nineteenth century after it was hit by lightning in 1870. The bells were cast in 1782, but there would have been bells before this date.

In 1640 the Rev. Richard Randes, Rector of Hartfield, founded a free school; the present school was built in 1842. A Parish Magazine of 1884 records that the school numbers have reached 164. The Rev. Edward Polehampton, rector and magazine editor from 1865 to 1886, records that the school was never so well attended, especially by children of five years old, this being the best time to start. A child coming to school at five, with regular attendance and attention, should be able to pass the last standard and leave soon after ten, and then add to the family's weekly earnings. Alice Crittenden was born in Hartfield in 1881 and lived at Castlefields; she left memoirs which recalled life in the village around 1887: 'Dresses were long, some with bustles. Some women wore bonnets, some hats. Sun bonnets for women and children were worn a lot as were black stockings. Men wore white cotton stockings for summer and woollen ones for winter; home-made leather boots were worn for school and work, also long and short leggings for men and boys. Elastic-sided and button boots were also worn. Celluloid collars were the fashion, also round-frocks for the men. When going to church, grey coats and skirts and little black bonnets had to be worn.'

194. The Lych Gate 1894

Lych comes from the German word leiche for a corpse; the pall bearers would rest the coffin on the post in the archway after carrying it across the fields. The Lych Gate is an old timber-framed house incorporating what was probably the priest's house and bears the date 1520, although this is thought to have been added at a later date. George Jenner, a carpenter and diarist who became the Parish Clerk in 1849 and was responsible for the restoration work of the Church after the fire damage, was born there in 1817. The Buckhurst Terrier of 1597, an estate map prepared for the Sackville estate to show property owned in the district by the Duke of Dorset, confirms that many houses in the village, especially those near the church, are medieval in origin.

195. The Keeys 1910

The Keeys came from Hever to set up a general building business in the village.

196 & 197. The High Street c1900

Mr Killick's grocer and draper shop was built around 1810; he kept his horses and cart for delivery service in stables which were on the site of the house now known as The Barn. In 1902 the village supported 3 Watermills, 2 butchers, a saddler, a forge, a fishmonger, bakers, grocers, 3 brickyards, a paper shop, cobblers and coal merchants. A scissor grinder can be seen in the left foreground. At the High Street end of Church Street stood a brick building called The Cage which was for the custody of prisoners prior to their appearing before the magistrate; this disappeared when the rural police were appointed and a new lock-up was built in the late nineteenth century.

198. The Anchor Inn 1895

The Hartfield Workhouse stood on the site of the Anchor Inn; an inventory dated 1777 states that it had a kitchen, a brewhouse, bakehouse, pantry, drink room and a back kitchen all downstairs, and what was called 'above stairs' contained eleven beds and three stedles. 'Without doors' was one well bucket and rope, one hog tub, one hoe, one trough and one hutch. There were twenty-five porridge dishes and thirty-six trenchers, ie wooden plates, but no mention of drinking cups. In 1841 there were forty-four inmates, all young girls under fifteen years of age, apart from one man and two baby boys. It had closed by 1861, when an agreement was made letting the premises to William Garrett, Wheelwright, at a yearly rent of £15.

199. Bolebrooke Castle 1900

The ancient mansion of Bolebrooke is said to be the earliest brick built house in the country, constructed by Sir Edward Dallingridge in the fourteenth century; a small part of it, comprising the entrance gateway flanked by two towers, is all that remains. Dallingridge was a nobleman who became the scourge of John of Gaunt and vigorously opposed his stewardship of the Forest until the latter appointed him Master Forester in the best poacher-turned-gamekeeper tradition. He later went on to build Bodiam Castle, and when his daughter, Margaret, married Sir Thomas Sackville, Bolebroke came to the Sackville family.

Wych Cross

Named for Richard de Wych (1197–1250) who became Bishop of Chichester in 1244, although the word wych is frequently spelt witch in early maps and records, Wych Cross was for many centuries a quiet and lonely staging post on the main London road, the old toll gatehouse stood by the main route which ran down to Chelwood Gate. Douglas Freshfield of Forest Row built Wych Cross Place around 1900 and fine gardens were laid out there by Gertrude Jekyll who worked at Nymans, Handcross; the estate of Ashdown Park was originally part of the Forest, enclosed under the decree of 1693 as part of the largest award which included Pippingford and Old Lodge.

200 & 201.
Wych Cross 1900

This photograph was taken at the junction of the Ridge and London roads.

On the Ridge Road looking east, Broadsdstone Warren is on the left hand side, with a small piece of National Trust land on the right.

202. The Pale 1908

A section of the ancient pale near Wych Cross shows the original ditch and bank which would have been surmounted by a fence to allow the deer to jump into the medieval hunting forest but prevented them from jumping out again.

203. High Beeches from Pippingford 1895

The ancient beech woods seen from Pippingford, with Ashdown Park in the left hand distance, the church of St. Richard de Wych visible through the trees on the right.

204 & 205. The Roebuck and the Toll House 1898

The Wych Cross to Lewes road, which ran through Chelwood Gate and Danehill, was turnpiked in 1752 and the old toll house was in the sharp angle between the Danehill and Nutley roads; a corner stone is all that remains of it today. Ponyfield Cottages are on the right, the old ale house on the left. The cottages and the pond in front of the white paling fence were demolished when Wych Cross house was built by Douglas Freshfield. The ale house was bought by Mr Thompson of Ashdown Park in 1883; as a league member of the church temperance society, he closed it down and it was used as a private house by his daughter and son-in-law. It re-opened as the Roebuck Inn in 1928.

206 & 207. Gypsy Camp at Rushy Bottom 1895

Rushy Bottom is the name of the straight piece of road that runs from Pippingford to Wych Cross, a misleading name for it lies not at the bottom but rather at the top of the ridge road which is now the A22. A parish report of 1869 records: 'On Ashdown Forest reside numbers of those strange people who come down to the villages and towns in houses on wheels or those large vans which comprise dwelling-house, shop and vehicle in one, the greater part of their rent and taxes being included in the cost of their hawker's licence. Their stock consists of toys, brushes and brooms of all kinds and all the paraphernalia of a fair; while another may be observed with rough ponies or donkeys and vehicles of the most primitive kind and construction, hawking heath and birch brooms and clothes pegs. Just before harvest, a motley group of men, women and children wend their way to the extensive corn tracts along the coast, intent on earning as much as they can at harvesting, for to this source they look for their annual supply of clothes.'

Convent of Notre Dame, Ashdown Park.

208. Ashdown Park 1912

Old records going back to 1822 show that rates were being paid on a house and lands on this site, when the property was owned and occupied by one Admiral the Hon. Jacob Henniker. He died in 1843 and the estate passed to his son, Edward; his widow lived at Old Lodge until her death in 1860. In 1867 Thomas Charles Thompson, MP for Durham, bought Ashdown Park, pulled down the original house and built a new, slightly smaller, mansion which was Victorian Gothic in character. A wealthy philanthropist, Mr Thompson employed a great many workers for his house and estate, dwellings were built for his employees, a school for their children and a church for worship; what emerged was almost a self-contained village. He also bought the Roebuck ale-house 'to stop his wife tippling'; she used to send the butler to the inn for supplies.

They had three children; the two sons died, one at eighteen, the other in infancy, and the church of St. Richard de Wych was dedicated to their memory. When Thompson died in September 1892, he left in his will money for black suits for each of his employees in order that they be smartly dressed for his funeral. His daughter, Mary, married the vicar of Forest Row, George Carnack Fisher, and they lived at the house known as the Roebuck. They had eight children, and it was their son, C.K.T. Fisher, who inherited the estate. An artist of considerable promise, he was killed in Palestine in 1917. During the First World War, Ashdown Park was used as a hospital and convalescent home for Belgian Army officers; in 1919, the estate was bought by a religious order, the Sisters of Notre Dame of Namur who remained there until 1971. It was, briefly, a branch of the International University of California, before Barclays Bank took it over as a training centre. Today it is a successful hotel, set in 186 acres of wood and parkland, complete with its own ghost, a lowly domestic nun who is said to haunt a room in the main block.

209 & 210. St. Richard De Wych c1910

Built in 1886, the church of St. Richard de Wych commemorated the Thompsons' two sons, Harold who died aged ten months, and Thomas More, who died of typhoid in Paris aged eighteen. Mr Thompson was a considerable churchgoer and it worried him that his employees had to walk four miles to worship at the nearest parish church in Hartfield so he built a private chapel, said to be a copy of a church in his native Durham, although the architect is unknown. The building was never consecrated and wasn't used after 1913 when the parish church at Coleman's Hatch was built. It fell into disrepair, vandals stripped the roof of lead and smashed the windows and it was eventually demolished in the late 1960s.

211. Beech Trees 1895

Chelwood Gate, Danehill and Birch Grove

Chelwood Gate was marked on the map of 1693 as Churwood Gate; the map shows how the Forest boundary would have extended westwards to the next gate in the pale known as Cowlers and eastwards to Brabies Gate, enclosing the medieval hunting forest which became two parts following the Decree of 1693 when 6,400 acres remained areas of common land and the remainder of over 7,000 acres became private land. Smaller commons were grouped along the edge of the Forest near villages, quite large stretches of common land to which tenants of the neighbouring Manors were to have access. However, many retained the rights they had within the Forest itself and they entered by the gates and hatches constructed in the pale.

212 & 213. The Red Lion c1895

The importance of the village pub one hundred years ago was paramount; travel and communication with the outside world was still difficult despite the improvements turnpiking had imposed upon the roads, and most people lived and worked in or around the village, so self-sufficiency was a fundamental tenet of life. Villagers were brought up to grow their own vegetables, rear their own livestock, mend their own boots, bake their own bread and brew their own beer, as well as make their own amusement. The development of the village pub, rather than the coaching inns opened for travellers of the previous generation, was greatly influenced by the Beerhouses Act of 1830 which permitted any householder assessed to the poor rate to retail beer and cider from his own house, on payment of two guineas, for consumption on and off the premises. The purpose was to popularise beer at the expense of spirits, particularly gin, and it led to a vast increase in the number of public houses in a very short space of time.

There was a cottage on the site of The Red Lion in 1669, occupied by one John Rolfe, and this is of interest because records would seem to indicate that it was built on the site of 'Churwood' Gate itself. In 1858, its tenant was described as a beer retailer, and it is first referred to as The Red Lion in an 1867 *Post Office Directory*, with William Turner listed as landlord. In the *Sussex Express* of July 1886, it was reported that Mr and Mrs Chatterton of Birch Grove Lodge, now Birch Grove House, celebrated their golden wedding with a dinner there. Today the symbol of the mythical red lion hangs from the inn sign, guarding the invisible entrance to a medieval royal hunting forest where kings no longer hunt and the Gate exists only in name.

214. Beaconsfield Road 1908

Joe Martin built the pillar box; the trees behind it were felled by troops belonging to the Portuguese army who were stationed here as a non-combative force during the First World War.

215. Stone Quarry Road 1896

The road took its name from an old quarry at the junction of the lane and Beaconsfield Road.

216. Stone Quarry Inn 1900

Stone Quarry Inn was at the northern end of the lane and was established some time between the enclosure of the area in 1864 and the 1871 Census, when John Walters was recorded as an agricultural labourer and beer seller. The freehold was owned by Charles Absolom, a brewer of East Grinstead, whose name appears on the cart in the yard. In 1878 Joseph Marshall took over as licensee and when he died in 1896, he was succeeded by his widow, Ansley (her name appears on the sign above the door) who remained there until 1925 which shows the acceptability of women as licensees. The name was changed in 1979 to The Quarry when the freehold was sold by the brewers; by 1984 it had closed down and the building was demolished to make way for new housing.

217. The Village Shop c1912

163

218. The Royal Engineers at Chelwood Gate 1912

The Royal Engineers were one of the many regiments who came to the Forest for manoeuvres in the summer of 1912.

219. Chelwood Beacon 1910

One of the most significant developments of the eighteenth century, and one that had a profound effect on rural areas, was the turnpiking of main roads which were privatised, improved and maintained by trusts who charged a toll to use the roads. Better roads enabled important

people to travel to and from their country estates to London; Edward Wormold was one of those who bought land on the outskirts of the Forest, and in 1882 he built a large period house, Chelwood Beacon. A philanthropic man, he provided money to build a mission hall and reading room in the village, and when the new church was built at Danehill, he donated a very fine organ. His residency was followed by Sir Harry Clarke Jervoise, who died in 1911, when the estate passed to the sixth Earl of Donoughmore, a distinguished politician; he was Chairman of Committees and Deputy Speaker of the House of Lords and served as Under Secretary of War 1903-05. During the First World War he served as a Colonel with the British Red Cross. A report in *The Courier* of the late 1940s reads: 'When the Earl was serving as an officer in World War I at Verdun, he was sheltering under a tree when a shell burst near him and a handful of chestnuts fell on his steel helmet. Putting some of them into his tunic pocket, the Earl planted them when next he visited Chelwood on leave. Today several thriving trees bear testament to this sentiment, which is commemorated by a small iron plate bearing the inscription: 'Horse chestnuts from Verdun Citadel 11th September 1917'.

The Earl died in 1948; since then Chelwood Beacon has been used as a residential home for the elderly.

220. Chelwood Common 1895

This photograph by Arthur Francis shows a view of the Common with Tanyard Lane running across the top of the hill and Boxes Lane in the middleground.

221. Pepper Alley 1898

Pepper Alley runs between Chelwood Gate and Danehill; Campbell's Rough is at the top of the ridge. The substantial kitchen garden would have provided fruit and vegetables for the families living in the cottages; another familiar sight at that time was the clothes line which has since disappeared from common land.

222. Danehill from Chelwood Common 1895

Danehill is really a forest village; its street once ran over a high hill but was diverted round the bottom during coaching days. The site is old, the name meaning 'denn' or pannage clearing in forested land, rather than anything to do with Norse burials. The church was built in 1892 on a high hillock and is approched by a very fine avenue of limes, the school building can be seen on the edge of the common by the track that ran through Pepper Alley linking the two villages.

223. Danehill Village 1910

This bird's eye view of the village is taken from the roof of the church, looking north and east to the distant Forest.

224. The Village 1895

Danehill's Baptist Chapel is on the left hand side of the road, an old alehouse, The Red Lion, is on the right. Now a private house called The White House, the crown post roof in the back section dates it to 1450; the imposing brick faced front section was added in the late 18th century. It was an inn serving one of the main roads from London to Lewes; the earliest record for a publican there is 1662. The diary of Giles Moore, rector of Horsted Keynes from 1656-79, records a number of occasions when he went to the inn to meet and pay the carrier who brought books down from London by pack horse train.

225. Danehill Old Church 1880

Known as Holy Trinity Chapel, the church was demolished around 1893 after the building of the new church was complete.

226. Woodgate 1910

In 1785 Peter Motley Hutchinson was paying Land Tax for Woodgate, a 'gentleman's house or hunting lodge' built on farmland he bought from the Yeomans and Warnett families, naming it after the old farm. Warburton Davies bought it from Hutchinson in 1817, and by the 1870s it had become the home of the MP, C.H. Corbett, with an estate extending up to Chelwood Gate. During the First World War it was requisitioned and became a Canadian Army billet; in 1949 it was bought by Cumnor House School, and it is now a thriving co-educational prep school with a dazzling reputation.

227. Corbett's Lake 1910

C.H. Corbett built a series of lakes down the valley between Danehill and Horsted Keynes during his tenancy of Woodgate, employing a small railway track to move the soil to create the dams, the trucks being pushed by hand; this one was on the opposite side of the road to where the school now stands and was sold off separately when the estate was broken up.

228. The Crocodile Inn 1910

The earliest use of the name, The Crocodile, is in the Court Books of the Manor of Horsted Broadhurst in 1864; the original building was built on waste in 1701 in the middle of the village, and was described in the will of James Luxford, dated 1847, as a beerhouse. In 1860 it passed to John Harvey of Lewes, a brewer, with William May as the tenant; the house was rebuilt in 1907 and the May family remained licensees until 1954. In the late 1980s it was closed and is now three private houses.

229. The Fire Pump 1910

The house fire in Church Lane required all hands to the pump, the water being drawn from the nearby pond. The pump would probably have belonged to Woodgate or Danehurst, two large local estates that would have afforded their own fire-fighting equipment.

230. The Hay Ride 1900

231. Faggot Stack, Birch Grove 1910

232. School Cross Road 1900

The two roads leading down to the right of the photograph lead to the two splashes of Twyford, hence the name which is derived from Two Fords.

233. Twyford Church 1910

The Church, which was also used as a school which gave the nearby crossroads its name, was built on private land. Part of the parish of Nutley, the vicar from that parish would take a service once a month. The building was demolished in the late 1950s.

234. Stumblewood Common 1904

Horses crossing the ford at Twyford.

235. Divall's Farm 1900

Divall's was a small working farm at the turn of the century. It was demolished in the 1950s by Lord Samuel who lived at Wych Cross Place.

236. Birch Grove 1900

Birch Grove is a hamlet, an oddity which grew up at a meeting point of the parishes of Maresfield, Fletching, Horsted Keynes, West Hoathly and East Grinstead. It remains much the same today as it did at the turn of the century.

237. Billings Cottage 1910

238. Ashdown Forest 1900

'In all English silvan landscape – taking landscape to mean not the foreground-picturesque of forest glades or undergrowth, but great wooded distances – there can hardly be anything richer than the view from the Forest Ridge southwards over the Sussex Weald. Its charm constantly has the addition of surprise; a gap in the roadside furze, or a gate between high hedges, gives a sudden outlook over the plain, rolling with swell and hollow to the grey rampart of the Downs which rise from it like island cliffs from the sea. At first sight it is all woodland: Anderida itself could hardly have stood thicker one thinks; but after a little looking the clearings, old and new, begin to show themselves – the squares of ploughland and pasture, the roofs of farms, the rusty scar of the quarry-hole, a windmill on a heathy common, that catches a travelling gleam of sun ten miles away, a haze of smoke drifting from a little town. The view unfolds itself, plane upon plane, every minute that it is watched.'

John Halsham: 'Old Standards – South Country Sketches'

174

BIBLIOGRAPHY

Historical Notes of Withyham, Hartfield and Ashdown Forest
by the Rev. C.N. Sutton 1902
A Portrait of Ashdown Forest by Roger Penn
The Sussex Landscape by Peter Brandon
Maresfield by Betty Turner
The Forest: Ashdown in East Sussex by Barbara Willard
Sussex by Barbara Willard
Have You Been Here Before? by Barbara Willard
Ashdown Forest by Garth Christian
Sussex by Arthur Mee
A Sussex Life: Memories of Gilbert Sargent Countryman edited by Dave Arthur
Maresfield Old and New by Rev. Ward Petley MA
A History of Ashdown House by Christopher Richmond
Ashdown Forest News, various issues
100 Years Ago in Hartfield (1992)
Hartfield Times, various issues
Forest Row Historical aspects and recollections, various issues
Danehill Parish Historical Society Magazine, various issues
A New Roman Road to the Coast by Ivan Margery
Sussex Notes and Queries Vol III No 3 & No 4
Leather and Cloth by M. Beswick
Sussex Archaeological Collections 81 (1940)
Sussex Archaeological Collections 112 (1994)
Tales of Old Sussex by Lillian Candlin
History of Sussex by M.A. Lower Vols 1 & 2
Nature in Literature by Edmund Blunden (Hogarth Lectures No. 9)
The New Oxford Book of English Verse
Bygone Crowborough by Malcolm Payne and Luther Batchelor
In Praise of Sussex by David Arscott
A Country Camera by Gordon Winter
Lark Rise to Candleford by Flora Thompson
Return of the Native by Thomas Hardy
East Sussex County Records Library, Lewes
Observations and Climate of Crowborough Hill (1890) by Dr C. Leeson-Prince
The Golf Courses of the British Isles described by Bernard Darwin (1910)
Royal Foliage by Molly Pears (1959)
History of the Parishes of St John the Evangelist, Heron's Ghyll by Father Philip Malden
Sussex of one hundred years ago by Aylwin Guilmant

The Society of the Friends of Ashdown Forest

Ashdown Forest is the largest single tract of open country in south-east England and one of the very few remaining areas of lowland heath left in Europe, supporting flora and fauna which are unique to this type of habitat. In order to maintain this important area of open heathland, the Conservators of Ashdown Forest employ a Forest Superintendent and Rangers whose task it is to care for the Forest. In 1961 a voluntary committee, the Society of the Friends of Ashdown Forest, was founded to assist the Board in its management and to encourage interest in conservation and peaceful enjoyment of the Forest. The Society was the brainchild of Ursula Ridley, a member of the Board of Conservators and one of the nine original committee members which included chairman R.J. Lumsden, the writer Barbara Willard, conservationist David Streeter, Nick Cranfield of Broadstone Farm, Arnold Silverstone (Lord Ashdown), Lord Dudley Gordon and Lady Dudley Gordon (later the Marchioness of Aberdeen), and it prospered from the start, soon becoming a registered charity.

The Friends were pledged to the support of the Conservators and over the years they have bought many items of equipment which help to run the Forest efficiently including a radio communications system, an excavator, a fire engine, a forage harvester, Ranger's van, the distance dial at Four Counties, picnic tables and a computer. Friends Clump was planted in 1973, the Year of the Tree, and when the Forest was put up for sale in 1987 by the late Earl De La Warr, a very large sum of money was needed to assist the purchase by the East Sussex County Council. The Friends joined with the Conservators in organising an Appeal that was magnificently successful. Since then they have helped the Conservators buy back private land within the ancient pale, gradually increasing the size of the Forest. A recent major purchase was that of sixty-nine acres at the Vachery, just north of Nutley, and adjoining Forest land.

You can become a member of the Friends by making a donation to the Society. In exchange you receive no special rights or privileges on the Forest but will receive copies of Ashdown Forest News and will be entitled to attend the annual general meeting. You will also gain the satisfaction of knowing that you are contributing to the maintenance of one of the most important open spaces in south-east England. Membership forms can be obtained from:

Ashdown Forest Centre
Wych Cross
Forest Row
East Sussex RH18 5JN